Bird Photography

Pure and Simple

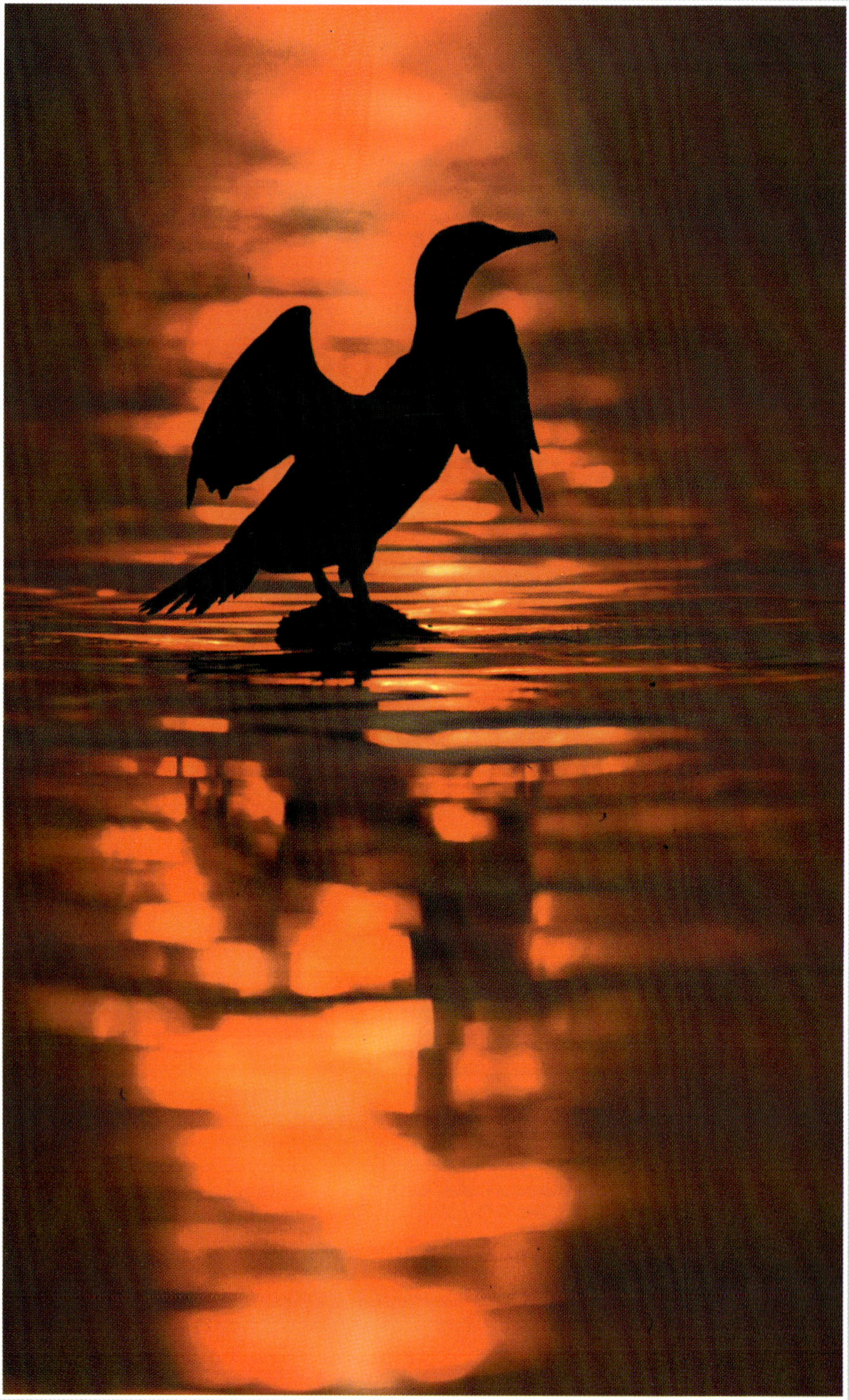

Bird Photography
Pure and Simple

by Arthur Morris

The Tern Book Company
New York

page ii
This Double-crested Cormorant was photographed in silhouette at the North Channel Bridge, Jamaica Bay Wildlife Refuge, Queens, NY.

Fuji Velvia pushed 1 stop, Canon FD 800mm f/5.6L lens & T-90 body, center-weighted average meter reading of red water plus 1/3 stop, set manually: 1/500 sec. at f/5.6.

BIRD PHOTOGRAPHY   PURE AND SIMPLE
 For information, address The Tern Book Company, 71 West 23rd Street, New York, NY 10010-4102

ISBN 1-890309-55-9

Library of Congress Cataloging-in-Publication Data

Morris, Arthur, 1946-
Bird photography : pure and simple / by Arthur Morris. -- 1st ed.
p. cm.
ISBN 1-890309-55-9
1. Photography of birds. I. Title.
TR729.B5M66 1997
778.9'32--dc21 97-30092
CIP

Printed in USA

First edition: September, 1997
10 9 8 7 6 5 4 3 2 1

Contents

In memory of my wife,

Elaine Belsky Morris,

who was my best friend and biggest supporter.
Her wonderful smile was lost to the world on
November 20, 1994.

Foreword

Photographing birds has been the driving passion in my life for the past 14 years. The thought of waking early and being afield with a tripod-mounted telephoto lens excites me even more today than it did in August 1983, when I purchased my first long lens, a 400mm.

Whether photographing Atlantic Puffins on a remote island off the coast of Maine, being frustrated by flitting warblers at Point Pelee, Ontario, or making images of Brown Pelicans on the cliffs of La Jolla, California, I, like all serious bird photographers, spend many hours at my task and come to know my subjects intimately. It is this intimacy that enables knowledgeable, prepared photographers to make not only artistically designed, technically perfect portraits, but images that depict spectacular action or private moments in the daily lives of their subjects.

In this booklet, I strive to share with you the knowledge that I've acquired and the techniques that I've used and developed, so that you may become that photographer. In the text, I mention the brand names of equipment that I have used and relied on for years. Though I strive to be fair and honest, the reader should know that I became a Canon contract photographer in April 1995 and continue in that role at the time of publication. I thank Canon USA for their past support and for sponsoring—in part—the printing of this booklet.

This booklet is designed to help you take better photographs, but in bird photography the results are often disappointing, and the experiences often frustrating, even for those with years of experience. Do not be discouraged. Read and re-read this booklet, especially the chapter on exposure, until the information becomes familiar; your work *will* improve dramatically.

I have no formal training in photography, art, or ornithology, so I feel privileged and extremely lucky to be able to make a living photographing birds.

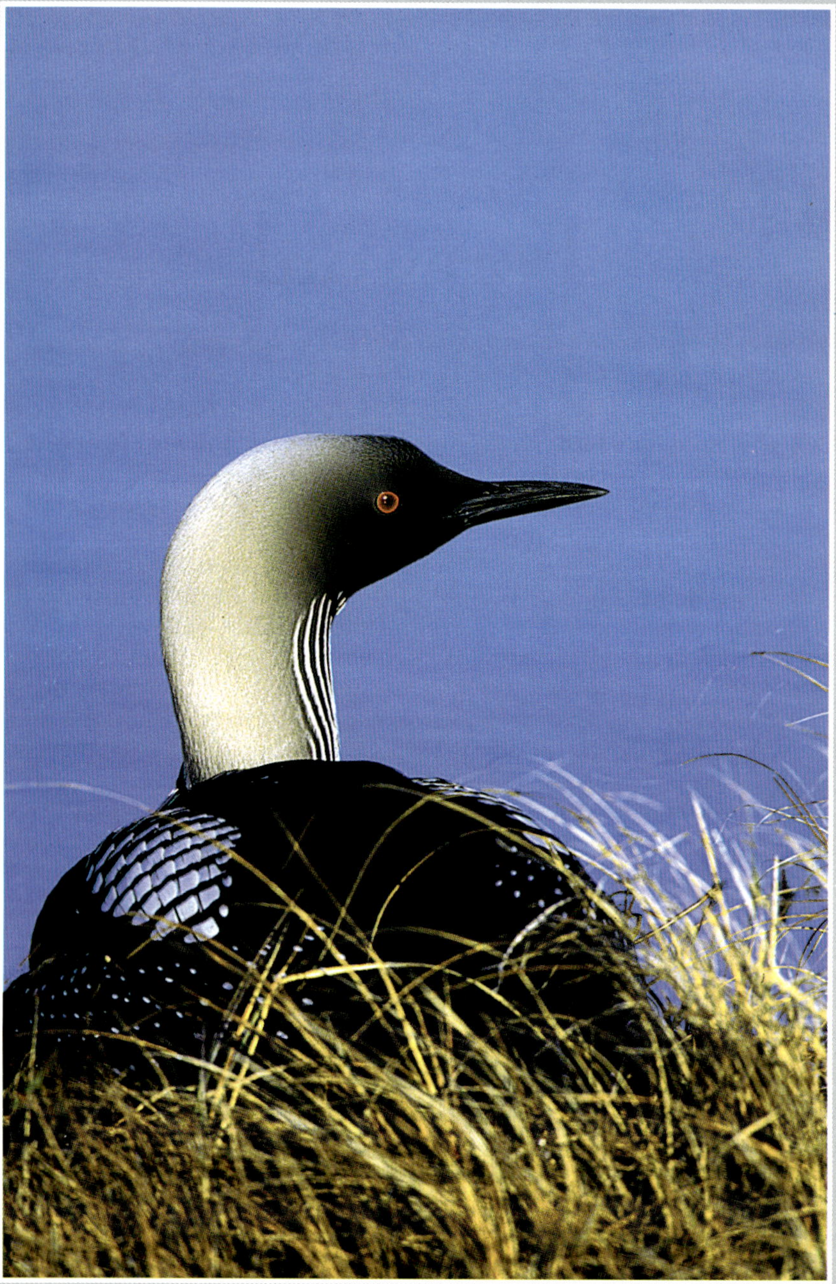

Pacific Loon on the nest at Churchill, Manitoba.

Fuji Velvia pushed 1 stop, Canon EF 600mm f/4.0L lens & EOS 1N body, 1.4X tele-extender, Evaluative metering at 0: 1/640 sec. at f/5.6.

Chapter I

Choosing and Using Equipment

Choosing a camera system and selecting a long lens today is a daunting and expensive proposition. "What is the best focal length? Should I buy autofocus or manual, new or used? Which is the best system? Is APO glass worth the additional investment? Should I change systems?"

Surely, you will want to research and test various brands before purchasing telephoto equipment. Read the product reviews in various photo magazines, consult knowledgeable camera store personnel, and speak to other bird photographers. Then buy the best equipment that you can afford.

In recent years, a quick look at the photo credits in prestigious wildlife calendars shows that the great majority of natural history images taken in North America were made with Canon or Nikon equipment. These systems are favored by nature photographers because of their reputations for quality and durability, because of the availability of a wide range of focal length lenses, and because they employ the latest in metering and autofocus technology.

Camera Bodies

Virtually all bird photographers choose and use 35mm single lens reflex (SLR) camera bodies as the basis for their photographic systems because of their light weight and the ease and speed of operation that they provide.

And while it is true that a camera is just a black box that lets in light, today's modern bodies offer a wide range of features that can make life a whole lot easier for nature photographers specializing in birds.

Several features that I consider indispensable are as follows:

Acceptance of Interchangeable Lenses

Point and shoot 35mm SLR cameras with fixed lenses are virtually useless for photographing birds.

Interchangeable Focusing Screens

Bright fine matte screens are your best choice; they make focusing easy. Split image focusing screens, standard in many camera bodies, will drive you nuts; avoid them at all costs.

Through-the-Lens Metering Automatic Exposure Control

All modern 35mm camera bodies offer TTL metering. By using automatic exposure mode in aperture priority, *you* select a lens opening (usually the widest) and *the camera* selects a shutter speed. You can work quickly while taking advantage of today's sophisticated metering systems.

Manual Exposure Mode

This feature, used extensively by many experienced photographers, allows *you* to select and set both the lens opening (aperture) and the shutter speed. I use it only in certain instances, such as when the sun is included in the photograph.

Power Winder

A power winder, or motor drive, is an absolute necessity for the bird photographer. With one, you will always be ready for the next shot or for long behavioral or flight sequences. Most modern camera bodies have built-in power winders.

Dial-in Exposure Compensation

In automatic exposure mode, this feature allows you to simply dial in exposure compensations— usually in $\frac{1}{3}$ or $\frac{1}{2}$ stop increments— as follows: plus (+) for lighter exposures, minus (-) for darker ones. Avoid camera bodies that have exposure compensation mechanisms that require you to use two hands or to take your eye away from the viewfinder.

Mirror Lock

This useful feature allows you to make photographs of static subjects at very slow shutter speeds by raising the mirror *before* making the exposure, thus eliminating vibration due to mirror slap.

Self Timer

At slow shutter speeds with tripod-mounted outfits, a self timer helps eliminate the vibrations caused by depressing the shutter button manually; sharper images result.

Depth of Field Preview

Viewing the image after activating the depth of field preview feature actually allows you to *see* the increases in depth of field as you set smaller and smaller apertures.

Autofocus

The ability of modern autofocus equipment to track moving subjects and attain accurate focus at the instant of exposure is science fiction-like indeed; for photographing birds that are flying, swimming, walking, or running it performs superbly. And for pho-

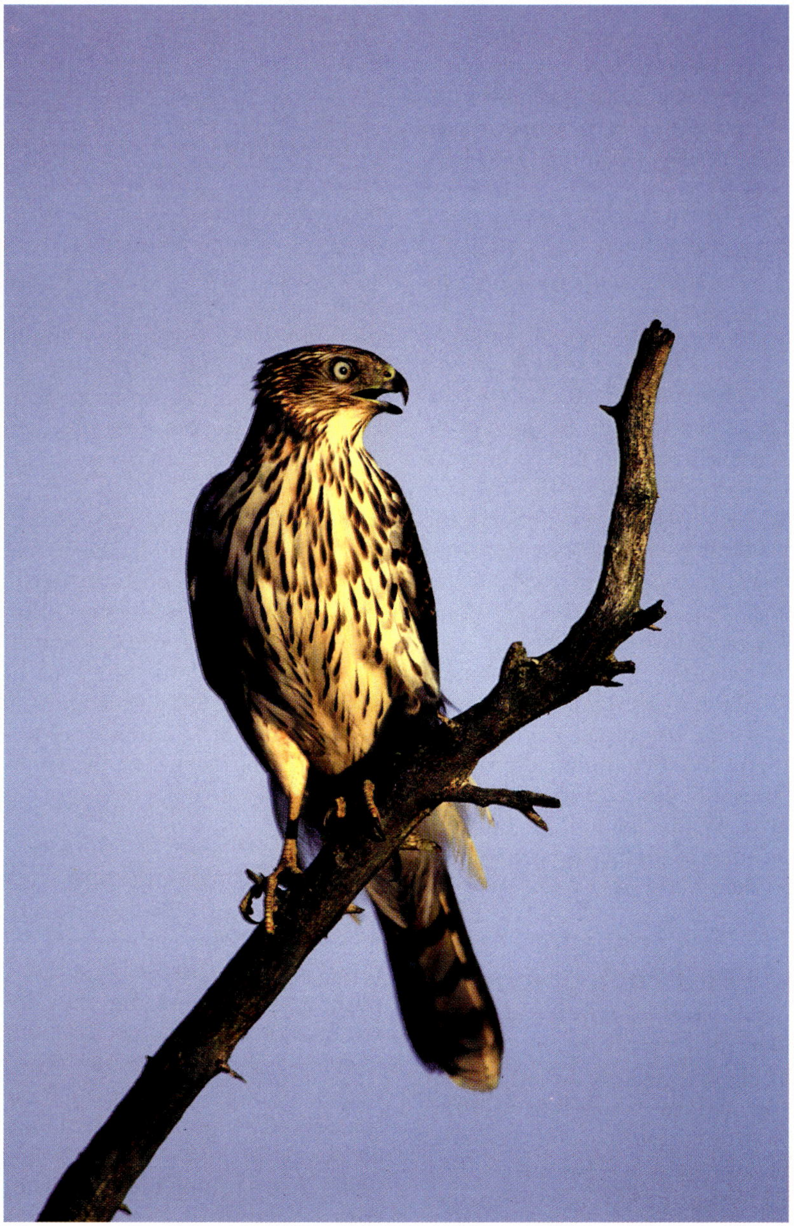

Motor drives allow you to make numerous exposures quickly when you are confronted by a handsome bird. This screaming juvenile Cooper's Hawk was photographed at Cape May, NJ.

Fuji Velvia pushed 1 stop, Canon EF 600mm f/4.0L lens & EOS 1N body, center-weighted average metering plus 1 stop: 1/320 sec. at f/5.6.

tographers with poor vision, it can be a godsend.

For photographing birds at rest (or other static subjects), autofocus offers absolutely no benefits at all to those with good vision. If you do opt for an autofocus system, make sure that you choose one with the focusing motor in the *lens*.

When in Doubt Read the Instructions!

There is one often neglected, invaluable accessory that comes with all camera bodies—the instructional booklet! Even if your camera body is *the most expensive on the market and offers every imaginable feature, it will be worthless unless you know how to use it.*

Study the instructional manual carefully. With the booklet open, load a battery, but not film. Mount a lens. Practice the various operations until they become second nature. When that male Painted Bunting lands nearby, you want to be ready.

Lenses for Bird Photography

What is *the* best lens for bird photography? Of course, there is no single *best* lens for all situations; serious bird (and other wildlife) photographers need a varied complement of lenses to help them capture on film the images that they have created in their mind's eye.

• • •

Now let's take a closer look at the different classes of SLR lenses, their uses in bird photography, and the factors that determine lens choice.

Wide Angle (17–35mm) and Standard (50mm) Lenses

Short lenses have limited uses in bird photography, but like bad little children, when they are good, they can be very, very good. Short lenses can be used for scenic shots with birds in the frame: "bird-scapes." They can also be used to photograph sky-filling flocks of waterfowl or smaller groups flying directly overhead at low levels.

Except when hand-feeding gulls (lie flat on your back while a friend feeds the gulls directly above you), opportunities for photographing wild, unrestrained birds at point-blank range with short lenses are usually few and far between, or far from civilization, where the birds may be unafraid of humans.

Short to Medium Telephoto Lenses (85–300mm)

Like wide angle and standard lenses, the lightweight lenses in this class can be useful at times for photographing birds, but they do not provide enough magnification to serve as everyday bird lenses.

For photographing a finch or sparrow at a window feeder, a tame owl in tight quarters, or a bossy pelican on a fishing pier, however, short telephotos can be ideal. They can also be used for flock shots of birds—either in flight or at rest—and for flight shots of individual birds at point-blank range. Some bird shooters get away with

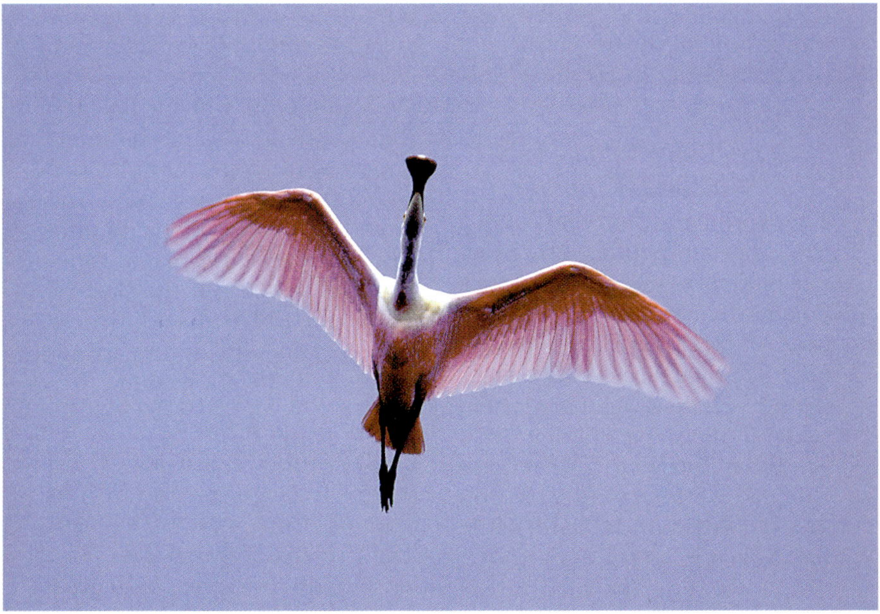

The Canon 400mm 5.6L lens/A2 body autofocus setup carried on a shoulder strap is light, easily handheld, and deadly on flying birds. This Roseate Spoonbill was photographed in soft afternoon light at Ding Darling NWR, Sanibel Island, FL.

Fuji Velvia pushed 1 stop, Canon EF 400mm f/5.6L lens and A2 body (hand-held), Evaluative metering plus 1/2 stop: 1/500 sec. at f/5.6.

300mm f/2.8 lenses and 1.4X and 2X tele-extenders (devices used to increase the effective focal length of a lens; they are also called multipliers or tele-converters).

Long Telephoto Lenses (400 and 500mm)

Many serious bird photographers choose their everyday bird lens from this group, most opting for either a 400 or 500mm focal length. These lenses offer enough magnification so that satisfactory image size can be obtained after a reasonably close approach is made. Additionally, long telephoto lenses produce lovely, soft, out-of-focus backgrounds.

Except for the fastest lenses, the f/2.8s and f/3.5s, the lenses in this class (especially the 400s) are light enough to be hand-held for flight photography. However, 300, 400, and 500mm lenses are long and heavy enough to demand the use of a tripod at all other times. But even when mounted on sturdy tripods, they are light enough to carry around for a full day in the field.

Some very good photographers prefer shoulder stocks (or "gun-stock" mounts), which are lighter than tripods and far easier to maneuver. I do not use them. The increased sharpness that comes with using a heavy-duty tripod and slow, fine-grained slide film should never be sacrificed if you are striving to produce high-quality images of birds.

Super Telephoto Lenses (600 and 800mm)

They cost many thousands of dollars. They are ponderously heavy and difficult to maneuver, yet fragile and delicate and, at times, in need of costly repair. Some cannot focus on nearby birds without the use of light-sapping extension tubes (hollow spacers that allow for closer focusing). All require the use of heavy-duty tripod heads and tripods. And while ball heads may *look* easy to use, simply locating the bird in the camera's viewfinder is a formidable task at first.

In spite of these and other disadvantages, relatively fast super telephoto lenses are awesome tools in the hands of experienced bird photographers. Their incredibly powerful magnification allows a photographer to stay well back from the birds and expose roll after roll without disturbing them. Distant birds are brought within range.

The relatively tiny Arca-Swiss B-1 Monoball head, rock-steady when locked up, yet smooth as silk at any tension setting, is a great improvement on the older, heavier models. With it, making small adjustments in framing and following slowly moving birds is—with a bit of practice—not too difficult.

By mounting an extension tube (or tubes, depending on the lens's minimum focusing distance) behind a super-telephoto lens to allow for closer focusing, most songbirds will fill half the frame, and head and shoulders portraits of large, cooperative birds, like gulls, are a snap. And those heavy-duty tripods, so difficult to lug around in the field, make it possible—if the bird remains perfectly still—to achieve sharp results with shutter speeds as slow as 1/30 of a second.

Lens Speed

By definition, a fast lens has a relatively large maximum lens opening. Conversely, a slow lens has a relatively small one. Fast lenses, with their great light gathering capabilities, allow the photographer to utilize relatively fast shutter speeds. They are extremely useful in the low light encountered at dawn or dusk. Today, the fastest telephoto lenses have maximum apertures of f/2.8 or f/3.5. Moderately fast ones have maximum apertures of f/4, f/4.5, or f/5.6. With slower telephotos, the largest lens opening may be f/6.7, f/8, or smaller.

Why opt for a slow telephoto lens when a faster one is available? The answer is simple: lots of pounds and lots of dollars! A Canon EF 400mm f/5.6L lens weighs less than 3 pounds. The Canon EF 400mm f/2.8L II lens weighs 13 pounds. And the latter lens costs more than five times the former. As a general rule for bird photography, I recommend choosing a longer, slower lens over a faster, shorter one.

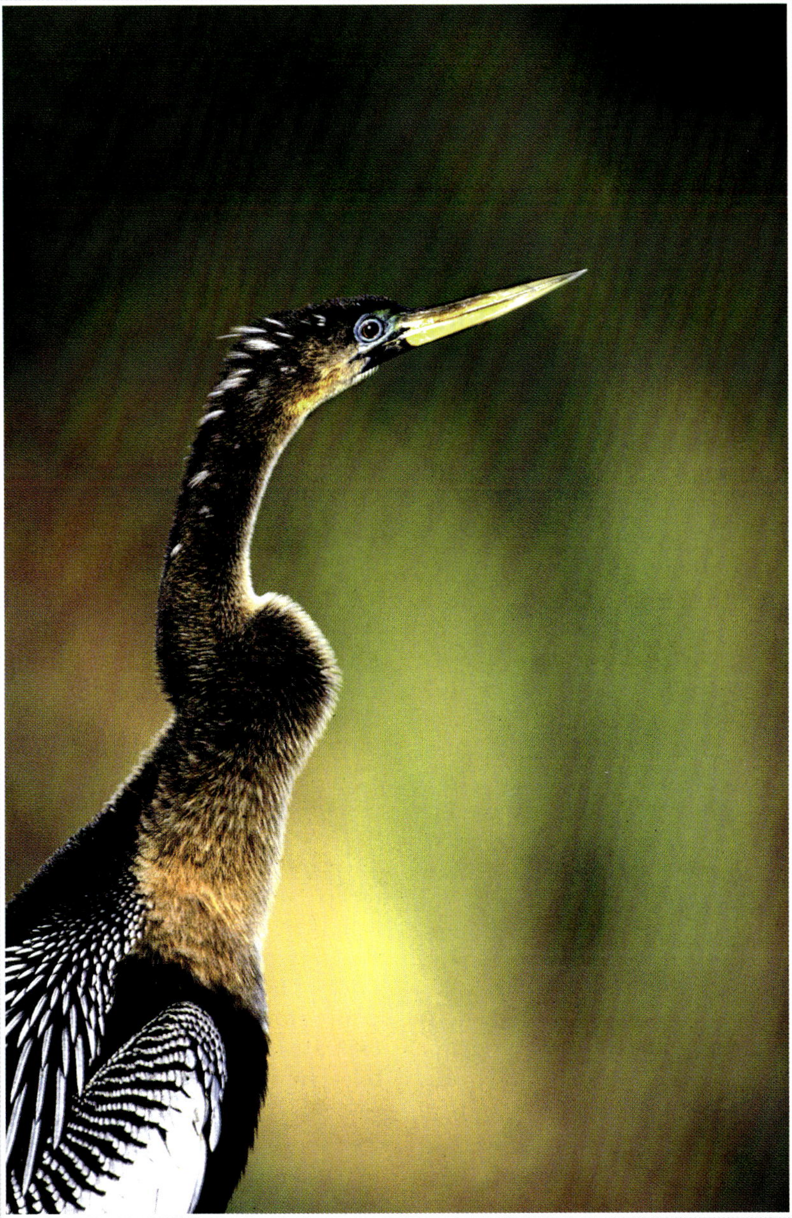

For many years I relied on the Arca-Swiss B-1 Monoball to support my long lenses. This female Anhinga in breeding plumage was photographed at Everglades National Park in Florida.

Fuji Velvia pushed 1 stop, Canon FD 800mm f/5.6L lens, T-90 body, & 50mm extension tube, center-weighted average metering plus 1/2 stop: 1/250 sec. at f/5.6.

What Brand?

There are no bargains when purchasing lenses; you get what you pay for. As stated earlier, Canon and Nikon are the overwhelming choice of North American nature photographers. Other top manufacturers, such as Olympus, Minolta, and Pentax, offer competitively priced, high quality telephoto lenses, and Sigma, Tamron, and Tokina now offer mid-priced quality lenses as well.

Beware, however, of off-brand telephoto lenses. Because of inferior optics, most are just not capable of producing acceptably sharp images. Many are slow lenses with minimum focusing distances so great that they can be used only to photograph very large birds at considerable distances; they cannot focus on birds that are anywhere near the photographer.

If extension tubes are used to allow for close focusing, vignetting, especially with the slower lenses, may occur: the corners of the photograph are darkened considerably. Do not buy *any* telephoto lens until you are positive that extension tubes can be used without causing vignetting. Lastly, lenses other than those of the highest quality will not produce acceptably sharp images when used with tele-extenders.

Glass Quality

Not even fast shutter speeds and huge, rock-solid tripods can produce razor-sharp images if your telephoto lens features inferior optics. The type and quality of glass used in the manufacture of a long lens is of utmost importance in obtaining critically sharp images.

The best modern lenses are specially constructed of glass impregnated with expensive elements. These lenses, called apochromatic (APO) lenses, are—unlike lenses made with standard glass—able to focus all three primary colors on a single plane. Thus, the resulting photos are sharper and do not exhibit chromatic aberration, a distortion of color, especially towards the edges of an image. Manufacturers designate lenses made with high quality glass with various codes including L, LD, and ED.

While choosing a lens made with high quality glass adds several thousand dollars to the cost of a telephoto lens, the difference in sharpness may be apparent only to those with highly trained eyes and powerful loupes (magnifying devices used for viewing slides on a light box). Lenses made with standard glass are capable of producing very sharp images, but will not perform as well as their more expensive cousins when used with tele-extenders.

Zoom Lenses

Lenses that can be adjusted to provide a continuous range of focal lengths are called zoom lenses. From 17–35mm wide angle zooms that fit in the palm of your hand to massive 150–600mm telephotos, zoom lenses can replace two, three, or more lenses. They are especially useful when working from fixed positions such as permanent blinds or parked vehicles. In all instances, they make it easy to frame a scene or a subject properly.

With recent improvements, modern zoom lenses are able to produce images almost indistinguishable from those taken with fixed focal length lenses, but the zooms are—in varying degrees—larger, heavier and slower than their fixed focal length counterparts. My favorite short zoom is the inexpensive Canon EF 28–105mm f/3.5–4.5 lens.

Mirror Lenses

Mirror lenses (cadiotropic lenses) are less costly, far more compact, and lighter in weight than straight telephoto lenses of the same focal length. They can easily be handheld and produce images of acceptable sharpness. But, because of several limitations, few top-notch bird photographers use them.

Most are relatively slow (f/8 or slower), necessitating the use of slow shutter speeds or fast film. All have fixed f-stops so that creative control of depth of field is not possible. Furthermore, points of reflected light in the background will appear on the slide as circular doughnuts.

Tele-extenders

Devices for increasing the effective focal lengths of telephoto lenses are called tele-extenders. For most camera systems, two are available: a 1.4X and a 2X.

The 1.4X increases the effective focal length of the prime lens by 40%, the 2X by 100%. With the former, one full stop of light is lost; two full stops are lost when using the latter. A 1.4X tele-extender transforms a 400mm f/4 lens into a 560mm f/5.6 lens. A 2X tele-extender converts a 500mm f/4 lens into a 1000mm f/8 lens.

Whenever you place a piece of glass between your quality telephoto lens and the film, image quality suffers. Additionally, with the increase in effective focal length comes an increase in the effects of camera shake and equipment vibration. Thus, slides taken with tele-extenders can—theoretically—never be as sharp as those taken with the prime lens alone.

With my Canon FD (manual focus) equipment, I had mixed results when using tele-converters, lots of soft slides with an occasional sharp image. At the same time, many others, especially Nikon users, swore by them. With my new Canon EF (autofocus) lenses, however, I am routinely able to make razor sharp images with both my 1.4 and 2X tele-extenders.

In general, the higher the quality of the prime lens, the sharper the image as long as the manufacturer's matched tele-extender is used. Increases in magnification and image size gained when using tele-extenders are significant.

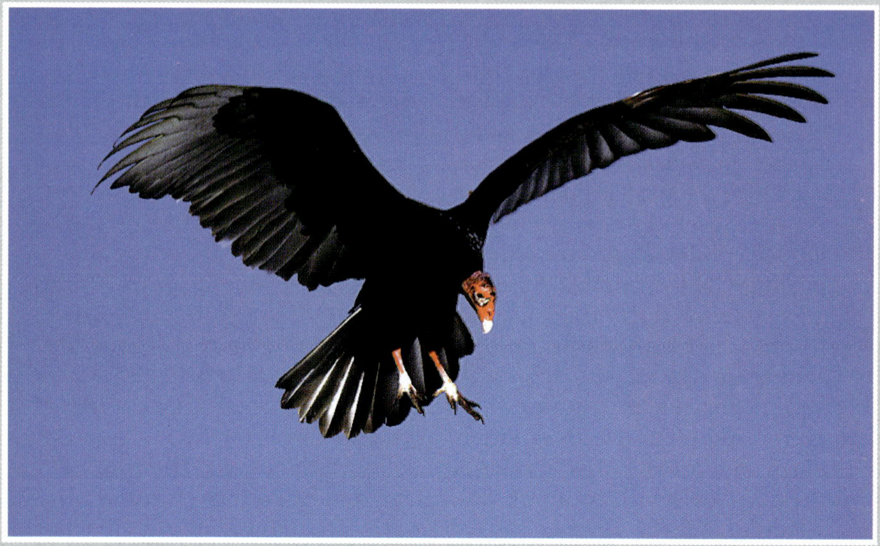

This Turkey Vulture was about to land on the green tin roof of the Visitor Center at Anhinga Trail, Everglades National Park, FL. Reflected light helped illuminate the bird's undersides.

Fuji Velvia pushed 1 stop, Canon EF 400mm f/5.6L lens and A2 body (hand-held), Evaluative metering plus 1/2 stop: 1/500 at f/5.6.

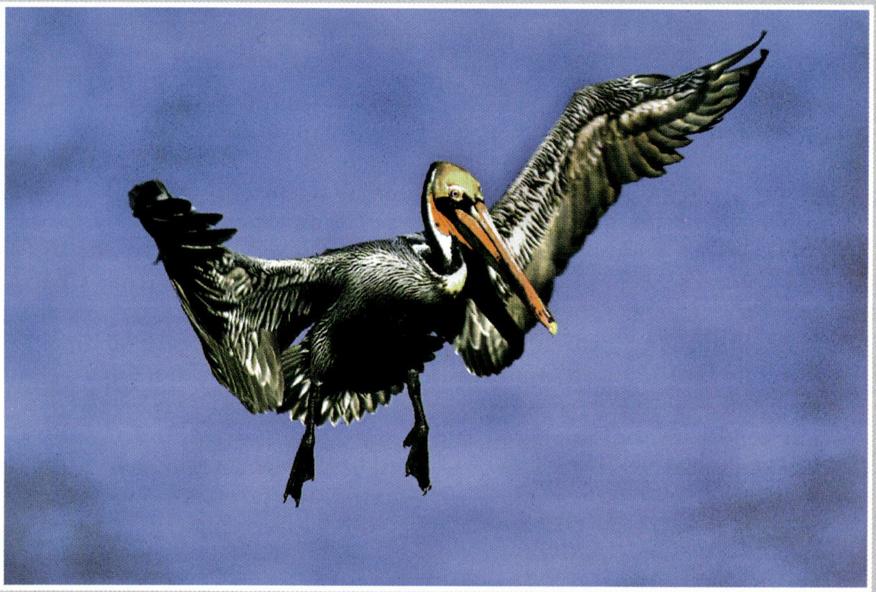

This Brown Pelican in flight was photographed from the cliffs at La Jolla, CA.

Fuji Velvia pushed 1 stop, Canon EF 600mm f/4L lens & EOS 1N body, Evaluative metering at zero: 1/640 sec. at f/5.6.

Chapter II

Autofocus

With manual focusing equipment, getting a single sharp flight shot on a 36-exposure roll was a great accomplishment; with Canon EOS bodies and EF lenses and to some degree, with other modern autofocus equipment, razor sharp images of birds in flight are now commonplace.

For photographers with poor or failing vision, autofocus is, of course, a virtual necessity. And even photographers with perfect vision will find that for shooting soaring red-tails, speeding roadrunners, swimming ducks, foraging sandpipers (and even running rhinos), today's autofocus equipment produces superb results on a consistent basis.

Autofocus Modes

Modern autofocus systems have two modes, one designed for photographing static subjects, the other for photographing moving subjects.

In the Canon system, the mode designed for shooting subjects at rest is called "One-Shot," in the Nikon system, "Single Servo." In either case, autofocus is activated by depressing the shutter button halfway. As long as the shutter button is not released, the point of focus will not change.

During workshop critiques, I see countless slides of dead-centered birds, which, for the most part, are compositionally boring. When questioned, photographers invariably answer, "But I use autofocus." (Many systems feature only a single focusing sensor located in the center of the frame, but the newest systems offer somewhat more compositional latitude; top-of-the-line bodies allow the photographer to choose one of several sensors.)

Off-centered Compositions

It is easy, however, to avoid centering a bird at rest in single-shot mode with *any* modern autofocus setup. Simply autofocus on the bird's eye by depressing the shutter button halfway, keep the shutter button depressed, *recompose*, and shoot. As long as the shutter button is not released, accurate focus will be maintained.

Focus Manually?

Some photographers, myself included, prefer to focus *manually* when photographing birds at rest. Simply flip the switch on the lens from AF to "M" for manual focusing, then focus on the bird's eye (using the *center* of the screen), recompose, and depress the shutter button.

Focusing manually eliminates the need to keep the shutter button depressed halfway. In addition, it is easier to fine tune the focus in response to slight changes in the subject's position. Remember: always focus on the bird's eye. When photographing distant subjects, focusing manually is a necessity; autofocus sensors can be deceived by heat shimmer.

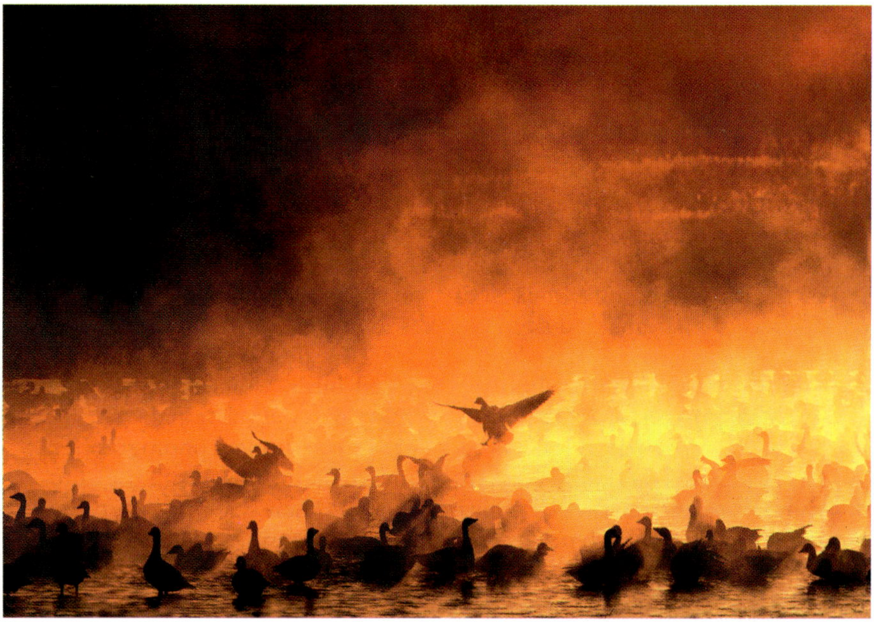

To photograph birds at rest, photographers with good vision should focus *manually*. This flock of Snow Geese was bathed in ground fog that was lit from behind by a rising sun in central New Mexico.

Fuji Velvia pushed 1 stop, Canon EF 600mm f/4.0L lens & EOS 1N body, Evaluative metering plus 1/3 stop: 1/800 sec. at f/5.6.

Photographing Flight and Action

The mode used to photograph moving subjects is called "AI Servo" in the Canon system, "Continuous Servo" in the Nikon system. The photographer must pan with the moving subject *while keeping the (active) focusing sensor* on the bird, depress the shutter button halfway to activate autofocus, and *keep the sensor on the subject* while keeping the shutter button depressed halfway to maintain focus.

Not to worry—this sounds more difficult to do than it is. After practicing—*without* film in the camera at first—you'll quickly get the hang of it. (Hand-holding a light 300 or 400mm lens is ideal for flight photography.) Images may be taken at any time by fully depressing the shutter button; most cameras will fire whether or not the subject is in focus.

The best autofocus systems calculate the speed and direction of the subject while tracking it and predict *where* the subject will be at the exact instant of exposure. (There is a time lag, measured in milliseconds, between the instant the shutter button is depressed and the time that the shutter begins to open.)

In due time, you'll find that tracking large birds that fly slowly and maintain steady courses becomes fairly routine. Small birds (like warblers and tanagers) and birds that fly erratically or at high speeds (like ducks and falcons) are extremely difficult to photograph in flight, even with the best modern autofocus equipment. But today, the limiting factor is the skill of the photographer rather than the ability of modern autofocus systems to track rapidly moving subjects.

When using the AF mode designed for moving subjects, the photographer becomes somewhat of a compositional slave to the technology. The autofocus sensor *must* be kept on the subject at all times. It is not possible to hold focus and then recompose (as it is when using a single shot mode).

As there is generally one best spot on the subject to place the sensor, it follows that there is generally only one possible composition. It is the technology that determines the composition.

The placement of the focusing sensor on the subject is of critical importance, especially when shooting birds flying or swimming by at close range. When shooting a fly-by gull, for instance, placing the central sensor on the gull's *body* will result in the sensor autofocusing on the near-wing when the near-wing is on the downstroke. Consequently, the bird's eye will be out of focus as the near-wing is closer to the film plane than the bird's eye.

A far better option is to attempt to place and hold the autofocus sensor on the bird's *neck*. Because the bird's neck and eye are very close to being on the same plane, the eye will be sharp. In addition, a more pleasing composition will result; the off-centered bird will have room to fly "into" the frame.

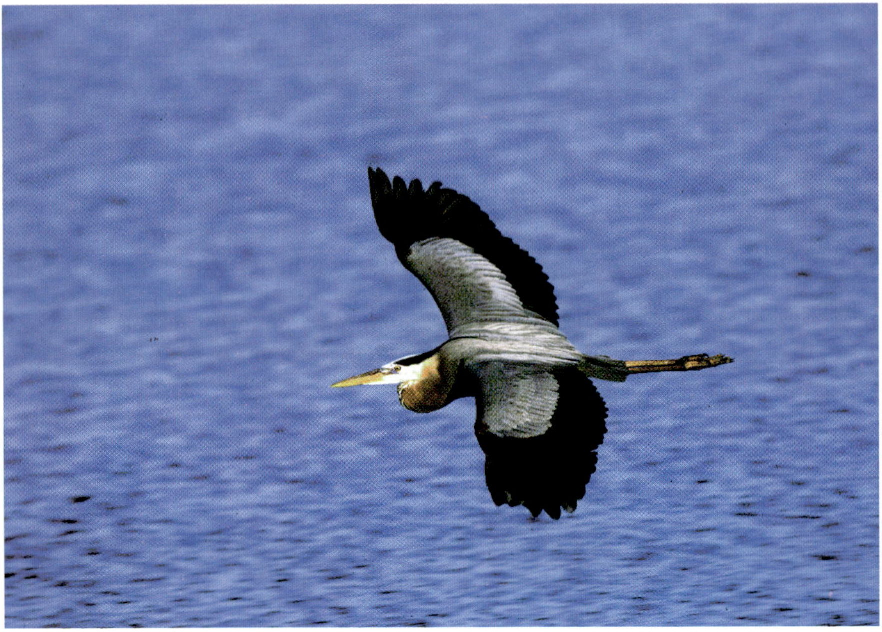

Placing the central focusing sensor on the neck of this Great Blue Heron resulted in a pleasing composition; Little Estero Lagoon, Fort Myers Beach, FL.

Fuji Velvia pushed 1 stop, Canon EF 400mm f/5.6L lens and A2 body (hand-held), Evaluative metering at 0: 1/500 sec. at f/5.6.

For birds flying, swimming, walking, or running directly at the camera, simply place the central focusing sensor on the subject's eyes, head, or neck and fire away; in nearly all cases the resulting dead-centered composition will be dramatic.

Autofocus With Tele-extenders

Generally, when using tele-extenders with autofocus telephoto lenses, autofocus will be maintained if the effective aperture is f/5.6 or larger. As with manual focusing equipment, a 1.4X tele-extender costs one stop of light, a 2X, two stops.

Mount a 2X tele-extender behind a 300mm f/2.8 lens and you'll have an effective 600mm f/5.6 lens; autofocus *will* function. But put a 2X on a 300mm f/4 lens and the resulting 420mm f/8 lens will *not* autofocus because the effective aperture, f/8, is smaller than f/5.6.

Chapter III

Exposure

Mount your long lens on a heavy-duty tripod and approach a beautiful bird with painstaking care. Compose a pleasing image that depicts the bird either in its natural habitat or against a background of pure color, focus accurately, and depress the shutter button. Does a great photograph result? Not always. If your image is over- or underexposed, your slides will wind up in the discard pile.

Exposure-wise, color slide film is quite unforgiving. Most slide films can tolerate a bit of underexposure, and my favorite, Velvia, a bit of overexposure. But in most cases, if you are off by more than one-half stop, the results will be unsatisfactory. (Color print film is much more forgiving; exposure errors of one to three stops can almost always be corrected during printing.)

The Basics

Shutter speed and *aperture* determine the amount of light that reaches the film. Each is measured in values called stops, which indicate a doubling or halving of adjacent values.

Shutter speed—usually measured in fractions of a second—is the length of time the shutter remains open. The longer the shutter stays open, the more light strikes the film. Shutter speeds commonly used in bird photography include 1/60 of a second (slow), 1/125 of a second, 1/250 of a second, and 1/500 and 1/1000 of a second (fast).

Each shutter speed in the series lets in half as much light as the one that precedes it, and twice as much as the one that follows. Most modern cameras offer shutter speeds in half-stop increments as follows (half stops in bold): 1/30, **1/45**, 1/60, **1/90**, 1/125, **1/180**, 1/250, **1/350**, 1/500, **1/750**, 1/1000, **1/1500**, and 1/2000.

The aperture is the opening that—when the shutter opens—

allows light to strike the film. Most lenses have adjustable apertures. The larger the aperture, the more light strikes the film. Each full f/stop lets in twice as much light as the one it precedes, and half as much light as the one it follows.

F/stops commonly encountered in telephoto photography are f/2.8, f/4, f/5.6, f/8, f/11, and f/16; f/2.8 is the *largest* opening in this series, f/16, the *smallest.* Many modern cameras allow settings in half-stop intervals as follows (half stops in bold): f/2.8, **f/3.5,** f/4, **f/4.5**, f/5.6, **f/6.7**, f/8, **f/9.5**, f/11, **f/13**, and f/16.

An exposure is simply the combination of a single shutter speed and a single aperture; together, they determine the amount of light that strikes the film. If the correct exposure in a given situation is 1/250 of a second at f/8, the same photo could be exposed for 1/500 of a second (half the exposure time) at f/5.6 (twice the light), or at 1/125 of a second (twice the time) at f/11 (half the light). In addition, there are many other shutter speed/aperture combinations that would let in exactly the same amount of light.

Opening up the lens means changing to a larger lens opening (a *lower* f/stop number). Stopping down the lens means changing to a smaller lens opening (a *higher* f/stop number).

Sunny Sixteen: *You* Determine the Exposure

On sunny days, you can determine the correct exposure *without* using your camera's meter by following the sunny sixteen rule: at the closest shutter speed equal to the fraction made by 1 over the film speed, an aperture of f/16 will give you the correct exposure for a middle-toned subject (against any background).

A middle-toned subject, by definition, is one that reflects 18% of the light that strikes it. A middle-toned gray is halfway between black and white. While photographers often refer to shades of *gray* when talking about middle tones, it is important to understand that all colors have middle tones. A middle-toned blue is halfway between dark navy blue and light pastel blue. A middle-toned red is halfway between deep fire-engine red and pale rose. And so on for each color.

For Velvia, 1/ISO = 1/50. The nearest shutter speed to 1/50 is 1/45 of a second. Sunny sixteen for Velvia is 1/45 at f/16, or 1/350 at f/5.6. Use the sunny sixteen exposure to photograph front-lit middle-toned subjects when the sun is at full strength (at least an hour after sunrise and no more than an hour before it sets on a clear day). When using the sunny sixteen rule, *your camera should be in manual exposure mode; you set the aperture and the shutter speed manually.*

To photograph brilliant white birds, stop down one full stop *(from the correct sunny sixteen exposure)*. Stop down $\frac{1}{2}$ stop *(from the sunny sixteen exposure)* for lighter than middle-toned birds. To photograph dark birds, open up $\frac{1}{3}$ to $\frac{1}{2}$ stop *(again, from the sunny six-*

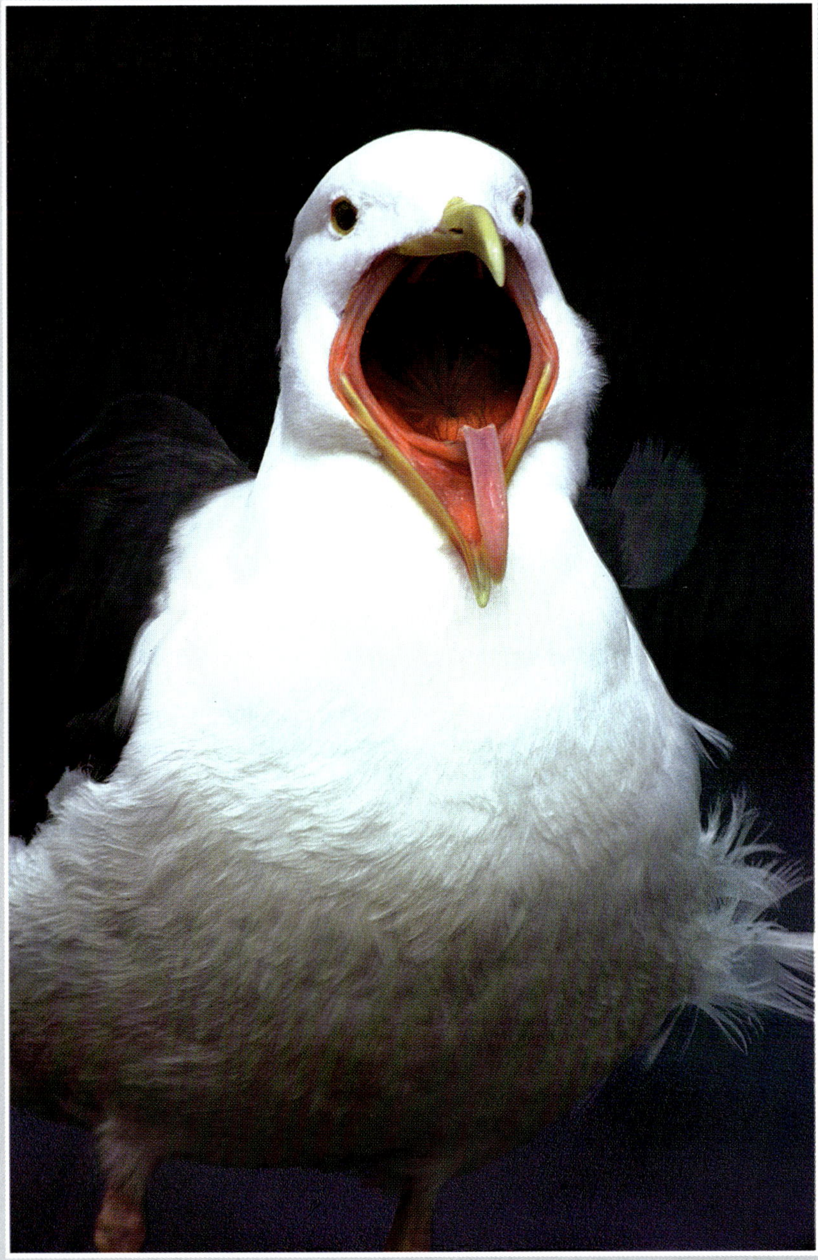

Spot metering the brilliant white breast of this yawning Western Gull and adding 1 1/3 stops of light resulted in a clean, bright white with good feather detail; La Jolla, CA.

Fuji Velvia pushed 1 stop, Canon FD 800mm f/5.6L lens & T-90 body, 75mm of extension, spot metered white plus 1 1/3 stops: 1/350 sec. at f/8.

teen exposure). And for black birds, open up from $\frac{1}{2}$ to 1 whole stop *(from the correct sunny sixteen exposure)*.

When using Velvia in sunny sixteen situations, photograph middle-toned subjects at 1/350 at f/5.6. Shoot brilliant white birds at 1/750 at f/5.6. Shoot light subjects at 1/500 at f/5.6. And shoot dark subjects at 1/250 or even 1/180 at f/5.6.

When using the sunny sixteen rule to determine exposure, calculations are made by your brain, not by the camera's metering system; compensations are made by adjusting the *sunny sixteen exposure* and setting the resulting values *manually*. Add or substract light by changing the shutter speed. Do *not* change the aperture and do *not* refer to your in-camera meter.

On days with less than full sun, you can determine a base exposure by taking a reading off a gray card (18% reflective gray cards are available at most photo shops) or any other object that you believe represents a middle tone: luxuriant green grass or tree bark that is neither *dark* brown nor *light* gray. Then, starting with the base exposure you have calculated, compensate for light or dark subjects as described above.

Checking Your Camera's Meter

The meters in most modern (electronic) cameras are generally very accurate. Meters in older camera bodies, however, are often off by a stop or more. Now that you understand the sunny sixteen rule, you can check your in-camera meter on a sunny, cloudless day (with no haze) as follows: mount a medium telephoto lens on your camera body; set the ISO to 125; select shutter priority and set the shutter speed to 1/125 of a second (that is, to 1/ISO); after making sure that your gray card is square to the sun, take a reading off it or off the clear north blue sky 40 degrees up from the horizon (a shade less than halfway from the horizon to directly overhead).

If your meter is accurate, the suggested aperture should be f/16 (as per the sunny sixteen rule). If your meter *is* off, you can calibrate it by changing the ISO setting until the meter correctly indicates an aperture of f/16. You will need to make a corresponding change *each time you load a fresh roll of film.*

For example, if you had to increase the ISO by one stop (from 125 to 250) to get an f/16 reading in your meter check, you'll need to increase the ISO one stop *whenever* you put a new roll of film in your camera. Likewise, if you needed to decrease the ISO by one-third stop (from 125 to 100), you'll need to decrease the ISO by one-third stop *each and every time you load a fresh roll.*

Another option is to return the camera body to the manufacturer and have the meter recalibrated.

Automatic Exposure Modes

With your camera in one of its automatic exposure modes, *it is the camera that suggests (and sets) the exposure.* Nearly all in-camera meters assume that the image they are metering averages to an overall middle tone, that is, that it reflects 18% of the light that strikes it.

When images average darker or lighter than middle tones, the in-camera metering systems will—in most cases—suggest incorrect exposures. With practice, however, you can learn how and when to override your camera's meter by making *exposure compensations,* that is, by adding or subtracting light from the suggested exposures.

Before learning to make exposure compensations, it is vitally important to understand the variety of metering patterns offered by your camera.

Center-Weighted Average Metering

For years, the center-weighted average metering pattern was standard in most SLR bodies, and most modern cameras offer it today as well. Center-weighted average metering reads the light reflected by the entire image, with an extra emphasis on the light reflected by the central portion of the image.

Spot Metering

Today, many—but not all—camera bodies offer spot metering as an option. Spot meters feature a tiny circle in the center of the viewfinder that usually comprises about 3% of the entire image. Simply point your lens so that the spot metering sensor lies directly on the area of the image to be metered. This area should be somewhat larger than the spot metering circle and of uniform tonality.

Segmented Metering Patterns

The latest modern camera bodies offer a variety of segmented metering patterns that go by a variety of names—"Evaluative" (Canon) and "matrix" (Nikon) among them. These metering patterns take exposure readings off numerous sectors of an image and then attempt to match them as closely as possible to the exposure readings of preprogrammed images. An exposure is then suggested and set.

Exposure Theory

In the explanation of the sunny sixteen rule, you will recall that various compensations were suggested for white, light, dark, and black subjects. What follows is a detailed explanation of exposure theory.

For perfect exposure of a front-lit, middle-toned subject, make the photo at the sunny sixteen settings in full sun (or at your base value settings in less than full sun).

For perfect exposure of a brilliant white subject, *subtract* one full stop of light *from the sunny sixteen exposure.* You are placing your brilliant whites at a level of one stop of underexposure (relative to the correct middle-toned exposure). If you photograph brilliant whites *at* the middle-toned exposure, your whites will be burned out, that is, considerably overexposed and detailless. By exposing whites *one stop darker than middle tones,* you will have clean, bright whites and will maintain feather detail. For a light (but not white) subject, subtract $^1/_2$ stop of light (for roughly the same reasons).

For perfect exposure of a black subject, *add* $^1/_2$ to one full stop of light *to the sunny sixteen exposure.* You are placing your blacks at a level of $^1/_2$ to 1 stop overexposure (relative to the correct middle-toned exposure). If you expose your blacks *at* the middle-toned exposure, they will be too dark and lack detail. For a dark (but not black) subject, add $^1/_3$ to $^1/_2$ stop of light (for the same reasons).

Center-weighted average and spot metering systems assume that everything in your viewfinder is, or averages to, a middle tone. If you meter a white wall or a black wall with either of these metering patterns and make the picture at the suggested exposure, your camera will render both walls as middle-toned grays. Your white wall will be too dark, your black wall too light.

To keep a white wall white (and overall light images light) you must open up or add light by using a *larger* aperture *than that suggested by your camera's meter* (while keeping the shutter speed

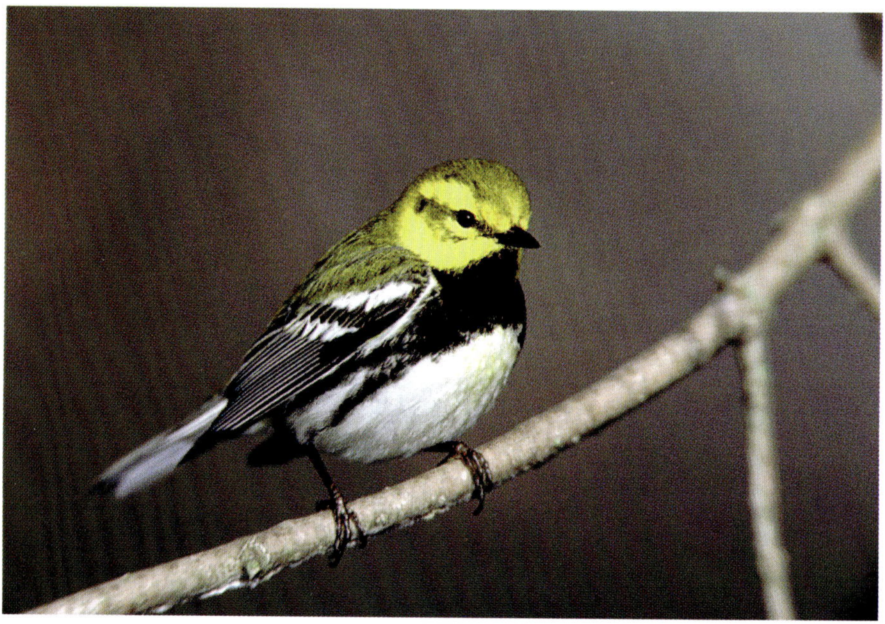

Trying to spot-meter a small, fast moving subject like this male Black-throated Green Warbler photographed at Point Pelee National Park in Ontario would be a futile endeavor. The image averages to an overall middle tone.

Fuji Velvia pushed 1 stop, Canon EF 600mm f/4L lens, 1.4X tele-extender, & 25mm extension tube, Evaluative metering at zero: 1/180 sec. at f/5.6. Fill flash at minus 1 stop.

constant). Alternatively, you could add light by choosing a *slower* shutter speed and keeping the aperture constant.

To keep your black wall black (and overall dark images dark) you must stop down, or subtract light by using a *smaller* aperture *than that suggested by your camera's meter* (while keeping the shutter speed constant). Or, you could subtract light by choosing a *faster* shutter speed and keeping the aperture constant.

By studying the above principles until you understand them completely, you will be well along the path to mastering exposure. Without understanding how to keep whites white, lights light, darks dark, and blacks black, you will be unable to master the use of your in-camera metering systems (no matter how sophisticated they claim to be) and you will be unable to determine the correct exposure on a consistent basis.

Making Exposure Compensations With TTL Metering

You are now ready to learn to make exposure compensations while using three types of in-camera metering systems.

Many photographers opt to make exposure compensations in their heads while working in manual mode; they turn rings or dials to set both the aperture and the shutter speed that they have calculated as being correct. I prefer to work in aperture priority/ automatic exposure mode and to *dial in* exposure compensation as required rather than to override manually.

I select an aperture (usually the largest), let my metering system select and set the exposure, and then change the exposure by dialing in compensation (if necessary). For more than a decade nearly all Canon camera bodies have allowed photographers to easily dial in exposure compensation in third or half stops *without taking their eye away from the viewfinder.* With most other camera systems, setting exposure compensations is more difficult, but other manufacturers are finally catching on.

I prefer automatic exposure with compensation to manually setting the exposure for several reasons: it is faster, especially when lighting conditions are changing rapidly, and I need only to manipulate the compensation dial (while my eye remains glued to the viewfinder).

Center-Weighted Average Metering With Compensation

For more than a decade this is the exposure system that I used and depended on, though for many years, I really did *not* have a thorough understanding of exposure theory. Center weighted average, *the* standard metering pattern for several decades, reads the light reflected by the entire image with an emphasis on the central portion.

With photos depicting birds that are small in the frame, your center-weighted average meter mainly reads *the light reflected by the background.* You must learn to control *the exposure of the background* in order to control the exposure of the subject. The larger the bird is in the frame and the more centered its image, the more effect it will have on the meter reading, but nearly all bird photographs include significant areas of background.

To learn to judge the tonality of an entire image (not just the bird) it can be very helpful to throw the image completely out of focus and ask yourself, "Overall, is this image darker than a middle tone, a middle tone, or lighter than a middle tone?"

If your answer is "darker," you'll come very close to a correct exposure by subtracting $\frac{1}{2}$ stop of light. If your answer is "a middle tone," take the photo at the metered exposure. If your answer is "lighter," you'll come very close to a correct exposure by adding $\frac{1}{2}$ stop of light. This approach helps to simplify a topic that can seem extremely complex at times.

Chart 1 details the center-weighted average with compensation exposure system that I developed and used successfully for more than a decade.

Spot Metering With Compensation

Many professional and advanced amateur nature photographers determine their exposures by spot metering and compensating. I do not, preferring instead to choose a metering pattern that reads the light reflected by the *entire image.*

Understanding spot metering with compensation, however, will greatly increase your overall understanding of exposure and will give you a way to cross-check exposures arrived at in the field by other methods.

For middle-toned birds, spot meter the bird if possible (or a large middle-toned object in the same light) and make the photo at that exposure.

For large brilliant white birds, or for birds with extensive areas of white, spot meter the white and open $1\frac{1}{3}$ stops. Brilliant white reflects roughly $2\frac{1}{3}$ stops *more* light than a middle tone, so opening up $1\frac{1}{3}$ stops will result in a one stop *underexposure* of the white—exactly what you want. Another option would be to spot meter a large middle-toned object and *subtract* one stop of light.

It is at this point that many photographers become confused. "First we're told to *stop down* one stop for whites, then we're told to *open up* $1\frac{1}{3}$ stop for whites. What's going on?" they ask. It is simply a matter of considering the *starting point. Stop down* one stop for whites *when starting at the sunny sixteen, gray card, base, or middle-toned exposure* to keep from burning the whites. *Open up* $1\frac{1}{3}$ stops *when starting at the spot metered exposure of a brilliant white* to prevent underexposure; remember: your in-camera meter wants to make everything gray.

For light lights, open up from $\frac{2}{3}$ to one stop from the spot metered exposure; for subjects just a bit

Chart 1. Center-Weighted Average Exposure Compensation Chart
(for medium-sized, off-center subjects)
Fuji Velvia
You may need to fine-tune these exposure compensations for your own film choice and equipment.

Middle-toned (MT) subject & background: Shoot the meter or $+\frac{1}{3}$. (Is Velvia a true ISO 40 film?)	MT background, MT subject	MT background, DK subject	Subject somewhat darker than the MT background: $+\frac{1}{2}$ or $+\frac{2}{3}$.
Dark (DK) subject, light (LT) background: +1 or $+1\frac{1}{3}$. Use +2 for extremes.	LT background, DK subject	F. DK background, DK subject	Dark subject, fairly dark (F. DK) background: $-\frac{1}{3}$ or $-\frac{1}{2}$. Use $-\frac{2}{3}$ or -1 for large black subjects.
Light or white (WH) subject against light background: $+\frac{2}{3}$ or +1.	LT background, LT/WH subject	MT background, LT subject	Large, light subject, MT background: shoot at the metered exposure.
LT/WH subject (or with WH highlights). MT background: $-\frac{1}{3}$ or $-\frac{1}{2}$. DK background: -1 or $-\frac{2}{3}$.	MT/DK background, WH subject	Any Background, Bright White subject	For large, brilliant white subjects, spot meter the white and add $1\frac{1}{3}$ stops.

lighter than a middle tone, open up from $\frac{1}{3}$ to $\frac{1}{2}$ stop.

Spot meter black subjects and subtract 1 or $1\frac{1}{3}$ stops of light, or else your in-camera meter will attempt to make them gray, that is, to overexpose them. Another option is to spot meter a large middle-toned object and then *add* from $\frac{1}{2}$ to 1 full stop of light.

For dark subjects, subtract $\frac{1}{2}$ to $\frac{2}{3}$ of a stop from the spot metered exposure; for subjects just somewhat darker than a middle tone, underexpose by $\frac{1}{3}$ to $\frac{1}{2}$ stop.

Whether you spot meter the subject and compensate, or spot meter a large middle-toned object and work from there, the idea is to place your lights at the appropriate level of underexposure and your darks at the appropriate level of overexposure. Chart 2 details these concepts and ties together the entire exposure package.

Segmented Metering Patterns

As stated earlier, evaluative and matrix type metering patterns mea-

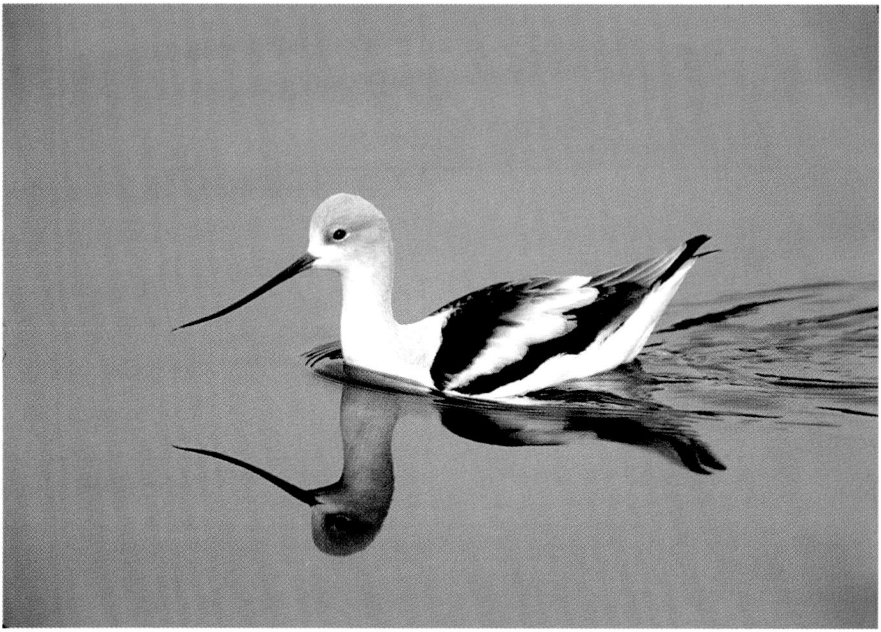

Adding two-thirds of a stop to the ambient (available natural light) exposure kept this overall light image light. This swimming American Avocet was photographed on a dull day at Newport Back Bay, California, with fill flash.

Fuji Velvia pushed 1 stop, Canon EF 600mm f/4.0L lens & EOS 1N body, 1.4X tele-extender, center-weighted average metering plus 2/3 stop: 1/250 sec. at f/5.6; fill flash at minus 1 stop.

sure the light reflected by numerous sectors of an image and then attempt to match these readings as closely as possible to the readings of preprogrammed images.

To take full advantage of these highly sophisticated metering patterns, it is my feeling that photographers must first master the basics of exposure and exposure theory because each manufacturer's segmented metering pattern will react differently to various lighting/subject/background combinations. When I first began using Canon's evaluative metering I had to learn how it reacted in different lighting situations with various subject/background combinations. I learned about my new metering pattern by comparing its performance to the performance of the metering pattern I knew best: center-weighted average. I would switch back and forth between the center-weighted average (with compensation) and the evaluative metering patterns.

If the exposure suggested by the evaluative system matched the exposure that I had arrived at with center-weighted average metering and compensation, then I knew that evaluative was doing its job,

CHART 2. UNDERSTANDING EXPOSURE THEORY

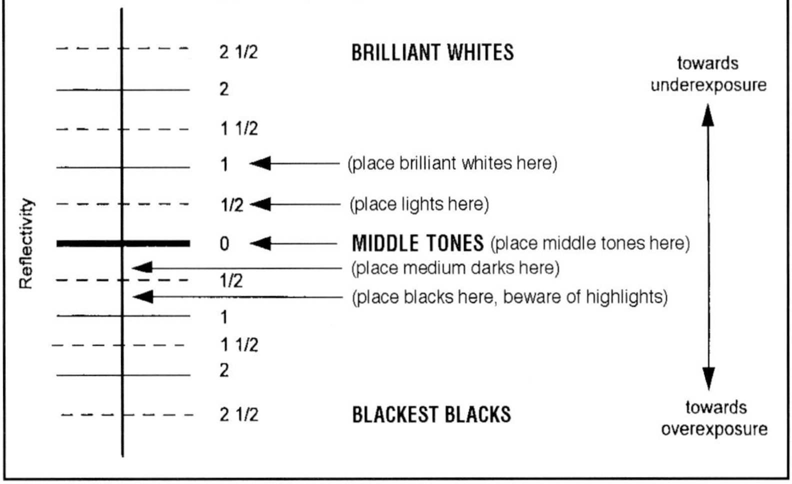

that it could be used in that one specific situation without compensation. If the readings did not match, then I knew that even the sophisticated evaluative system would need my help (in the form of exposure compensation) in *that specific situation.*

When photographing birds in flight or birds against light or reflective backgrounds, Canon's Evaluative metering pattern performs superbly in bright sun; the camera recognizes the bright conditions and adds from $\frac{1}{2}$ to $1\frac{1}{2}$ stops of light. In low light, however, *the photographer* needs to add light, just as when working with center-weighted average metering. In most lighting conditions, Evaluative metering opens up as needed for fairly large subjects that are darker than the background; you, however, will need to underexpose a bit for dark backgrounds. And you will need to learn how *your camera's* segmented metering system performs in different lighting conditions to use it effectively.

Final Thoughts on Exposure

Learn the basics. Practice judging the tonality of a variety of both subjects and backgrounds. Learn to use center-weighted average metering with compensation. Learn the characteristics of your camera's various metering patterns. In the field, use several methods to determine an exposure and then cross-check the results. Choose and stick with one film, and learn its characteristics. In the beginning, take good field notes. You'll soon be coming up with satisfactory exposures on a consistent basis.

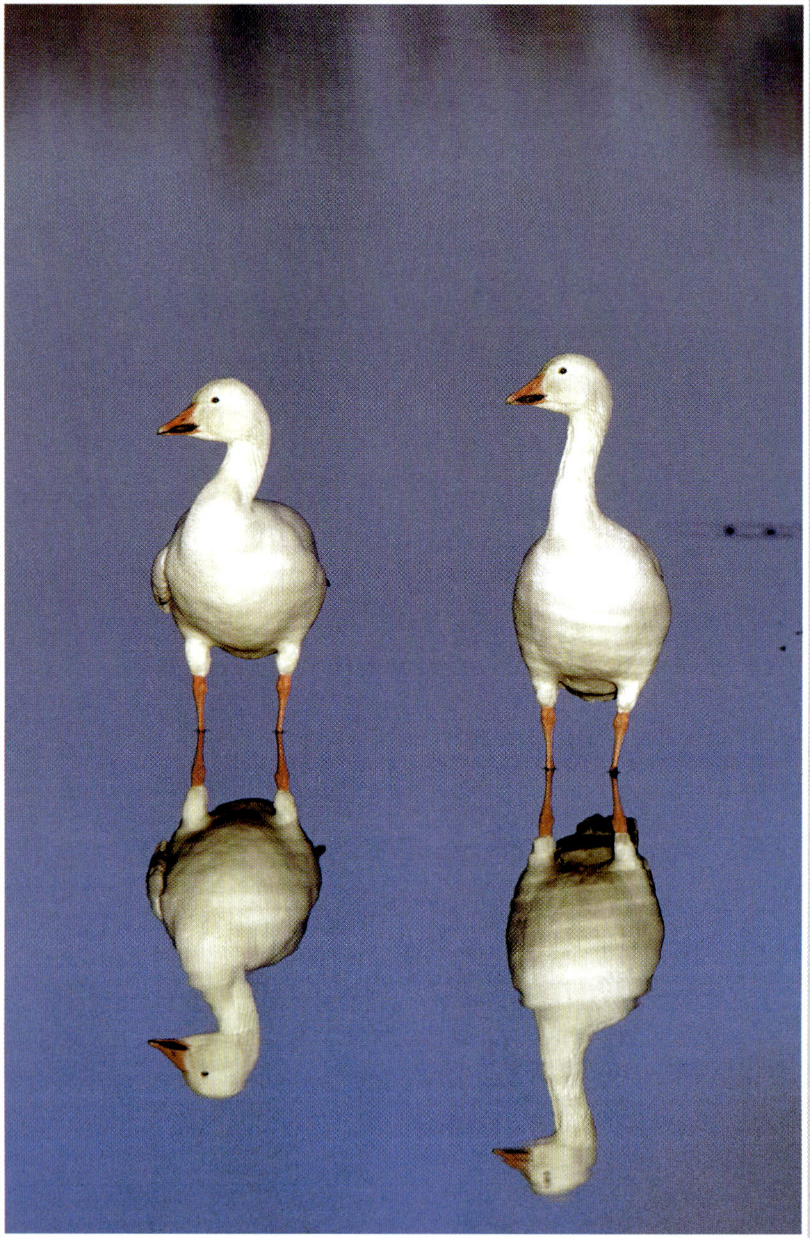

Noted bird artist Julie Zickefoose calls late afternon sunlight "butter light." It adds drama to any image. This mated pair of Snow Geese was photographed in central New Mexico at Bosque Del Apache NWR.

Fuji Velvia pushed 1 stop, Canon EF 600mm f/4.0L lens and EOS 1N body, Evaluative metering minus 1/3 stop: 1/400 sec. at f/8.

Chapter IV

The Qualities of Natural Light

On sunny days, the warm light of early morning and late afternoon, rich with red and yellow components, is preferred for bird photography to harsh midday sunlight. Colors are enriched and textures enhanced when lit by sunlight striking at a low angle; contrast is reduced as well.

The light of midday, with more blue components, is less pleasing; direct overhead sunlight is generally to be avoided, especially when photographing white birds; this light is harsh and creates unpleasant shadows. But all rules are made to be broken—one of my favorite (and best selling) photos, of a singing Common Yellowthroat, was photographed under a glaring sun at 12 noon!

On light overcast or cloudy–bright days you can photograph birds all day long. These conditions produce a lovely, soft, even light that reduces contrast. Misty or foggy mornings can produce similar light and dramatic results as well; in general, open up 1 stop in fog (or your images will be underexposed).

On cloudy–dark days, the use of fill flash is practically a must. To use fill flash, first set the exposure for the ambient (available natural) light, and then set your flash between minus $\frac{2}{3}$ and minus $1\frac{2}{3}$ stops (or 0 or minus $\frac{1}{3}$ stop for black subjects). I set my Canon 540EZ at minus 1 for most middle-toned subjects. Fill flash will add a highlight to the eye, restore color balance, and bring dead images to life. Ideally, when using fill, the use of flash in the photograph should not be obvious.

I use a fresnel flash multiplier (designed to concentrate the flash beam) called the Better Beamer/ Walt Anderson Flash Extender

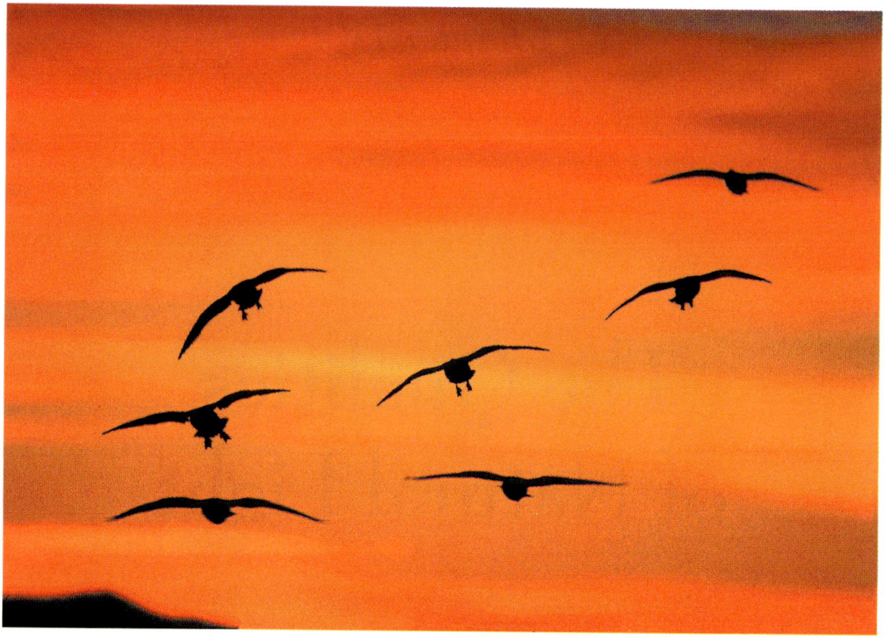

With small-in-the-frame subjects, like these Snow Geese at Bosque Del Apache NWR, NM, silhouettes are a snap; overexpose from 1/3 to 1 full stop depending on the brightness of the background. Framing was done with great care.

Fuji Velvia pushed 1 stop, Canon EF 600mm f/4.0L lens & EOS 1N body, Evaluative metering plus 2/3 stop: 1/30 sec. at f/4.

(see BIRDS AS ART under Suppliers). It folds flat for storage, is sturdy yet extremely lightweight, easily assembled, and very effective. Flash output is increased by more than two stops. This saves battery power, allows the use of a smaller aperture, or allows you to photograph at greater distances.

Strongly backlit subjects can easily be photographed in silhouette; yellow, orange, pink, purple, and violet skies at sunrise and sunset create dramatic backdrops, as do their watery reflections. *If the sun is not in the photo and the subject is not large,* simply take a center-weighted average meter reading of the image and open up from ½ to 1 stop (depending on the brightness of the background.)

If the sun is in the frame, meter the adjacent sky or its reflection in water, and then *set that exposure manually.* If you do not follow these steps, your in-camera center-weighted average meter will stop the lens down drastically and you'll wind up with a black sky.

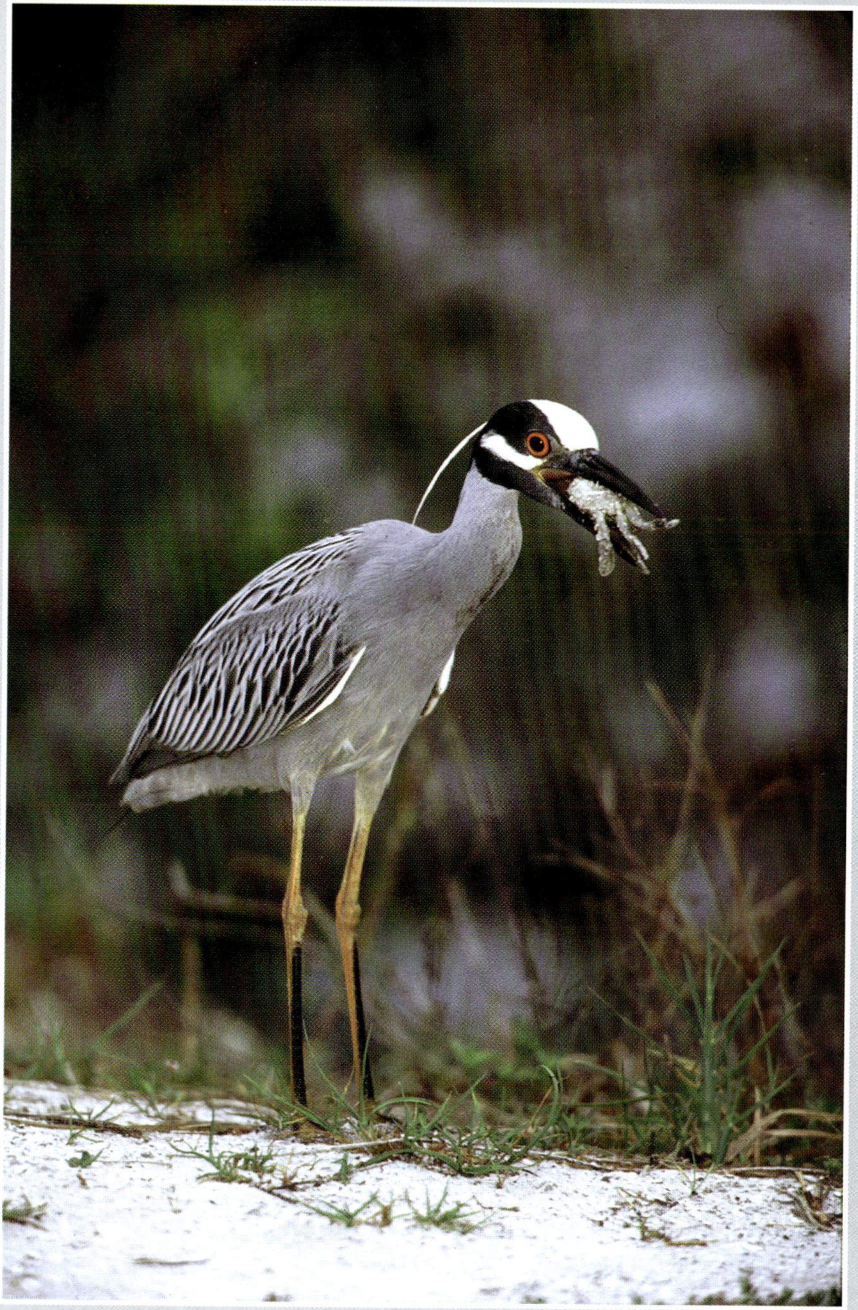

A touch of fill flash restored color balance and brought this image of a Yellow-crowned Night-Heron to life; Ding Darling NWR, Sanibel, FL.

Fuji Velvia pushed 1 stop, Canon EF 600mm f/4.0L lens & EOS 1N body, Evaluative metering at 0: 1/350 sec at f/4, fill flash at minus 1 1/3 f/stops.

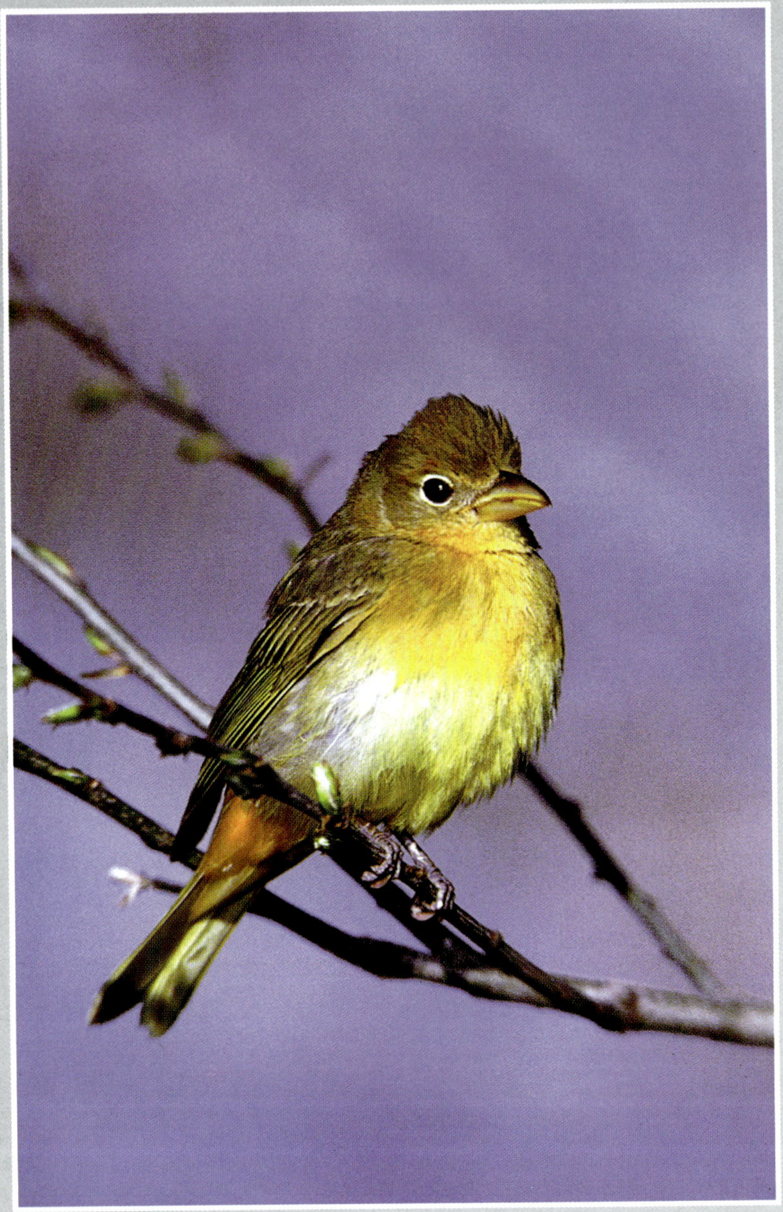

Fujichrome Velvia pushed one stop is my everyday film. It offers fine grain, superb sharpness, excellent resolution, clean whites, neutral grays, black blacks, and a vivid color palette. This female Summer Tanager was photographed at Point Pelee, Ontario, as it rested after crossing Lake Erie.

Fuji Velvia pushed 1 stop, Canon EF 600mm f/4.0L lens, EOS 1N body, 1.4X tele-extender & 25mm extension tube, Evaluative metering plus 1/3 stop: 1/640 sec. at f/5.6.

Chapter V

Film Choice

Choosing a film is a personal decision, and there are lots of great films available today, so the choice is a difficult one. If you are just starting out, you need to learn a few basics, and then do some homework.

The Basics

A film's speed, which indicates its sensitivity to light, is, like aperture and shutter speed, measured in stops. ISO 100 film is twice as sensitive to light as ISO 50 film, and half as sensitive as ISO 200. Readily available films whose ISO numbers fall on full stops include 25, 50, 100, 200, and 400 ISO film. (ISO 64 film is $\frac{1}{3}$ stop faster than 50 ISO film.)

The slowest films (ISO 25, 50 and 64), offer extremely fine grain. The faster films (ISO 200 and 400), allow the use of relatively fast shutter speeds, even in low light, but show a bit more grain. ISO 100 films offer a fine middle ground, and are the choice of many nature photographers today.

Why Color Slide Film?

Most—but not all—nature photographers choose a relatively slow color slide film as their workhorse film for a variety of reasons:

1. Films in the ISO 50–100 range offer fine grain that allows for successful enlargement, while offering enough speed to shoot on sunny, cloudy–bright, and even cloudy days.
2. Since birds are colorful creatures, most photographers choose color film over black and white film. The results with the latter can, however, be quite artistic.
3. The cost of color slide film and processing is far less than that of color print film and developing.
4. Prints (and color separations for publication) can easily be made from color transparencies (slides).

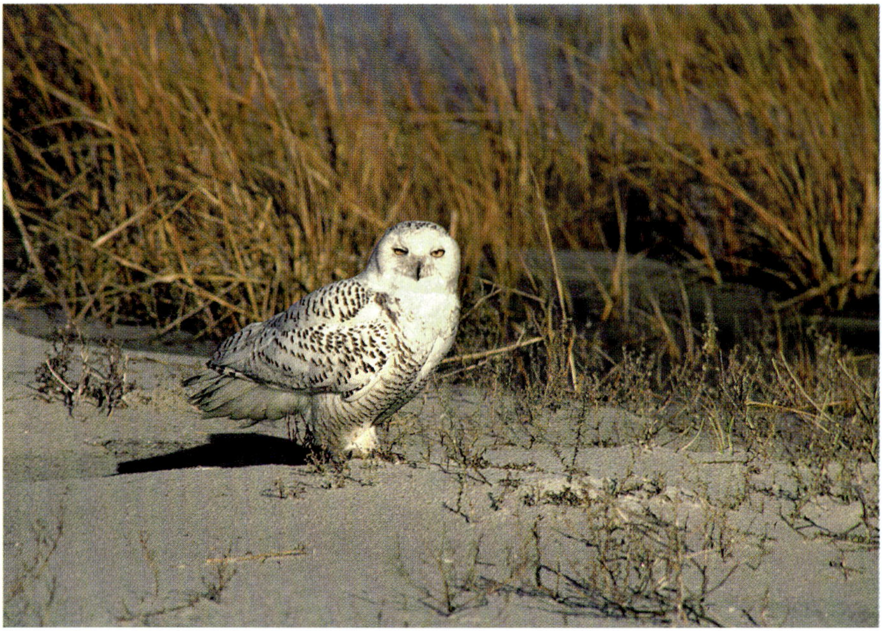

For decades, Kodachrome 64 was *the* standard color slide film for nature photography. This Snowy Owl was closely approached at Jones Beach, Long Island, NY.

Kodachrome 64, Canon FD 400mm f/4.5 lens & T-90 body (shoulder stock), base exposure minus 1/2 stop: 1/500 sec. at f/5.6.

In September of 1991, after using Kodachrome 64 for nearly eight years, I shot a few rolls of Fujichrome Velvia (ISO 50) and was amazed by its incredibly rich and vivid colors, its ability to capture countless shades of green and brown, its sharpness (which rivals or exceeds that of Kodachrome 64), and its incredible performance in low light. Velvia quickly became my everyday film and remains so to this day. Other popular slide films in use today include Fuji Sensia and Provia, Ektachrome 100S and 100SW, and Agfachrome RSX 100.

My advice is to take a careful look at the various color slide films in use today; if at all possible, examine *original* slides or shoot a few test rolls of the films that you are considering—duplicates or magazine reproductions do *not* accurately depict a film's qualities. Then pick one film with qualities that you like and stick with it exclusively for at least one year. By doing so, you will learn the film's characteristics, qualities, and idiosyncracies. Once you come to know and understand your film well, it can better help you to express your individual photographic style and vision.

Chapter VI

Image Sharpness

Pleasingly composed, well lit photos of strikingly beautiful birds are—in most cases—nothing if the image of the bird is not sharp, or better yet, razor sharp. Photographs of moving birds taken at slow shutter speeds can, however, yield blurred, yet highly artistic images.

Image sharpness is a function of the following six factors.

Lens Quality

The higher the quality of the glass in a telephoto lens, the sharper the resulting image—period. And that goes double when using tele-extenders.

Accurate Focusing

If you do not focus your long lens accurately, unsharp photos will always result. Take your time and use extreme care when focusing on the bird's eye and on the feathers surrounding it.

Bright matte focusing screens make focusing easier, as do fast lenses. All modern lenses feature wide open viewing, so the same image will appear brighter through an f/4 lens than through an f/5.6 lens. The brighter the viewfinder image, the easier it is to focus.

Shutter Speed

The faster the shutter speed, the less the blur due to equipment vibration. As a general rule, bird photographers should choose the fastest possible shutter speed that lighting conditions and film speed allow. Do this by working in aperture priority and choosing your lens's largest opening.

You can (as I almost always do) gain an extra stop of shutter speed by pushing your film one stop. After loading the film, *double* the film's ISO; see your camera manual for details. When the roll is finished, be sure to write "Push

+1" on the film cassette with a black marker. Lastly, tell your lab to push-process that roll one stop (or else the whole roll will be one stop underexposed). In short, to push a roll of film, lie to the camera and tell the truth to the lab.

Aperture (lens opening)

Large apertures (signified by low f-stop numbers such as f/2.8, f/4, and f/5.6) *minimize* depth-of-field. Depth-of-field is the range in front of and behind the point of focus that is in reasonably sharp focus. When using large apertures to photograph nearby birds, the foreground and background will be thrown completely out of focus. In most instances, this is desirable; your backgrounds will be soft and beautiful. Different parts of the same bird, however, may not be in focus.

Small apertures (denoted by high f-stop numbers like f/11, f/16, and f/22) *maximize* depth-of-field. Shooting at small apertures increases the range of sharp focus.

As a general rule, I recommend shooting wide open at all times *unless* you have a good reason to stop down, that is, to choose a smaller aperture. The number one good reason for stopping down is to ensure enough depth-of-field to cover the subject, to ensure that *all parts* of the bird are in sharp focus. Remember, however, that choosing a smaller aperture necessitates the use of a slower shutter speed, and slower shutter speeds often result in a *loss* of sharpness due to equipment shake. If in doubt, choose a faster shutter speed over a smaller aperture.

Note: if your camera has a depth-of-field preview feature, activating it will allow you to *see* the changes in depth-of-field as you set smaller and smaller apertures.

Equipment Shake

It's a fact, long lenses shake. At shutter speeds slower than 1/125 of a second, these vibrations often cause soft (blurred, unsharp) images. When making long exposures, the slap of the mirror as it snaps up and out of the way (to allow the light to hit the film when the shutter opens) causes vibrations that can result in unsharp images.

The most effective way to reduce equipment shake when using a large telephoto lens is to use a heavy duty tripod and a rock-solid ball head. My current choices are the Gitzo 410 tripod and either the Wimberley head or an Arca-Swiss ballhead.

Many top professionals strongly recommend the use of an electronic (or other) cable release to minimize camera body shake for all types of nature photography. When it comes to bird photography, I strongly disagree, preferring instead to depress the shutter button with my index finger.

Holding the camera body gives you a feeling of total control, a feeling that the camera (and lens) are an extension of your

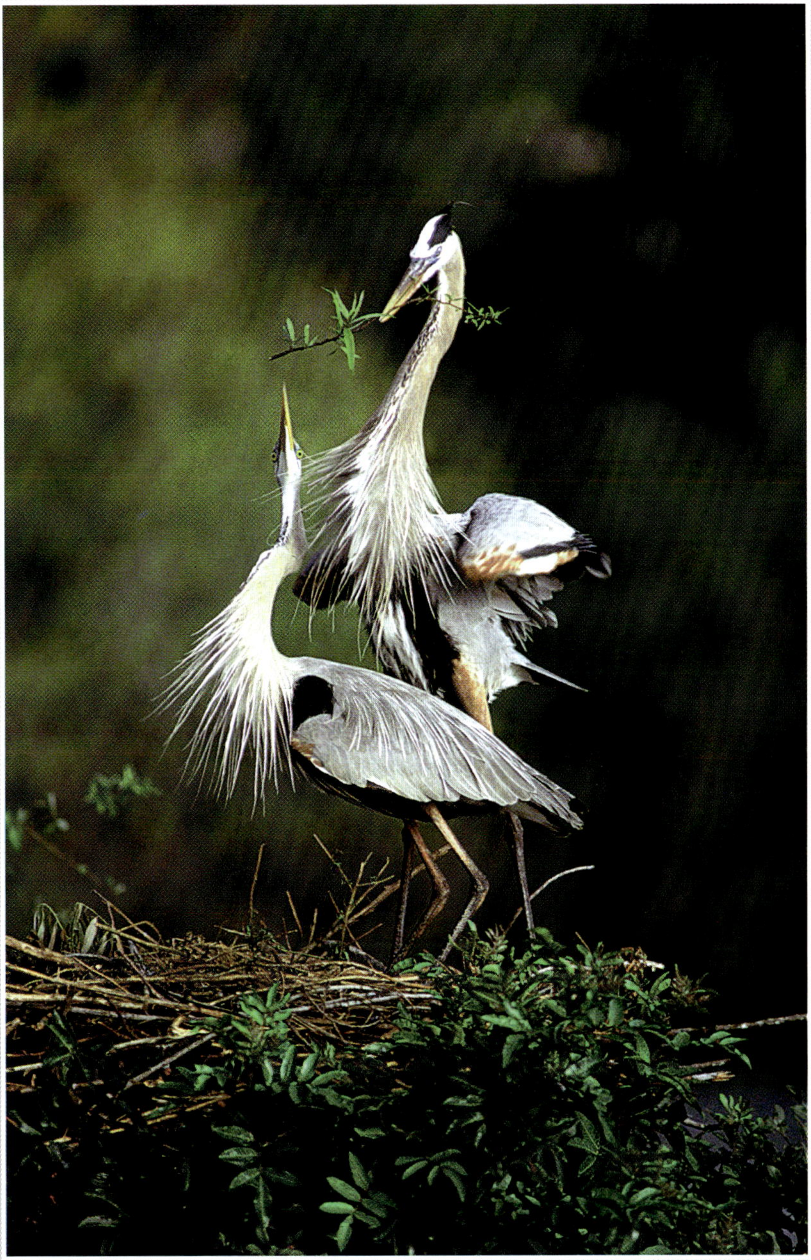

Working wide open throws distant backgrounds pleasingly out of focus. This Great Blue Heron courtship image was made at the Venice Rookery, South Venice, FL.

Fuji Velvia pushed 1 stop, Canon FD 800mm f/5.6L lens & T-90 body, center-weighted average metering minus 1/3 stop: 1/500 sec. at f/5.6.

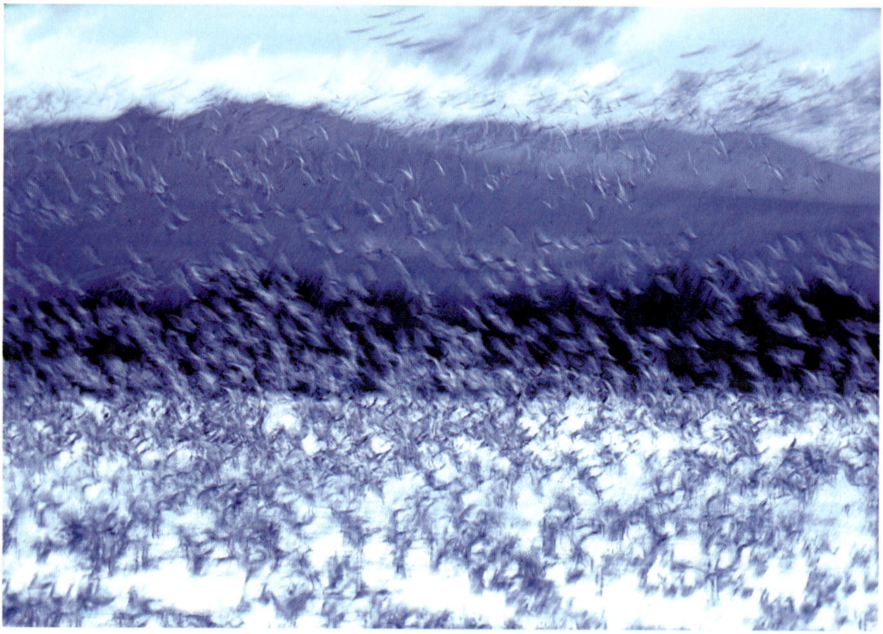

This necessarily blurred image of Snow Geese lifting off on a cloudy morning at Bosque Del Apache NWR, NM, was made at the fastest possible shutter speed: 1/15th of a second.

Fuji Velvia pushed 1 stop, Canon EF 400mm f/5.6L lens (tripod-mounted) & A2 body, center-weighted average metering plus 1/2 stop: 1/15 sec. at f/5.6.

body. You are far better able to get in tune with the rhythm of a bird's movements and to make minute adjustments in framing and composition. For added sharpness, steady the lens by placing your left hand on top of the lens barrel directly over or just forward of the tripod head, and press your cheek against the back of the camera.

Subject Movement

To reduce blur due to subject movement, choose the fastest possible shutter speed (by selecting your lens's largest aperture). At 1/1000 of a second or faster, almost all motion will be frozen. At 1/750 or 1/500 of a second, most movement will be frozen; images of fast flapping birds may exhibit blurred wingtips. At 1/350 and 1/250 of a second, some blurring of moving birds may occur, and with shutter speeds of 1/125 of a second or slower, blurring will most likely occur.

To create blurred images that accentuate motion, choose relatively slow shutter speeds of from 1/2 to 1/125 of a second. This technique can work well, especially with birds in flight, but producing successful images on a consistent basis is difficult; experimentation is necessary.

Chapter VII

Composition

While being born with an artistic eye is a plus for all photographers, designing pleasing images of natural history subjects is a skill that can be learned and then developed and enhanced over time. When I first began photographing birds I plunked every bird dead center in the frame.

In 1984, I signed up for an eight-session introductory nature photography course offered by the New York City Audubon Society. The instructor, Milton Heiberg, taught us the basics of composition in a single evening. He did a superb job of answering this beginner's question: "Where *do* you put the bird?"

When "putting" the bird in the frame, of course, you do not actually move the bird—wouldn't that be nice? Simply shift your camera up or down, left or right. Shifting the camera upward will move the bird down in the frame; shifting it a bit to the right will move the bird left in the frame, and so on and so forth.

Horizontal Composition

Thumb through a field guide. It's easy to see that most birds are horizontally oriented. Most are two to three times wider than they are tall. If you get close enough to such birds to fill more than half the frame, you should choose a horizontal format.

Rule of Thirds for Horizontal Composition

When a bird's image is small in the frame, divide the frame into thirds both horizontally and vertically. Place the subject—in this case the bird—at one of the four points of intersection. By placing the bird at one of these four points, you give it room to move in the frame, room to see, room to fly.

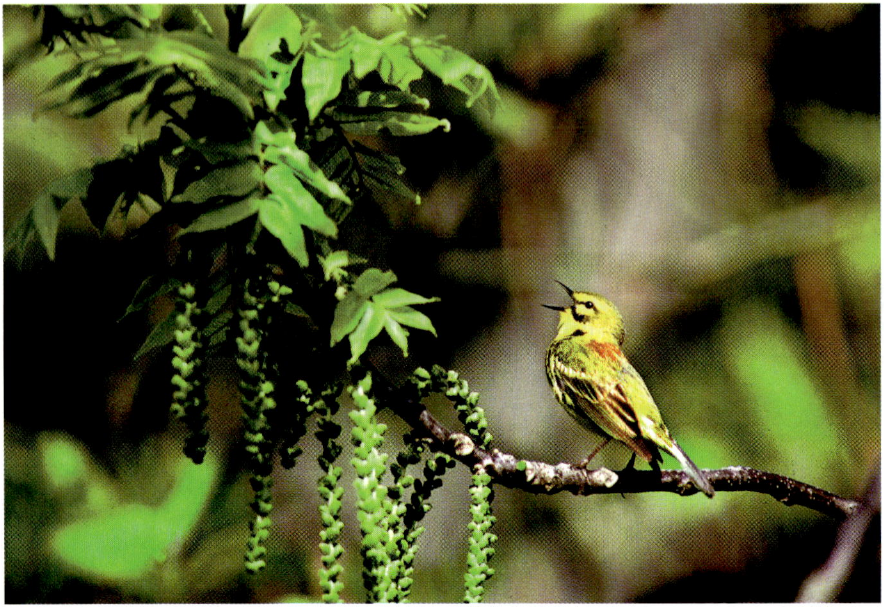

With small-in-the-frame subjects in attractive habitat, the rule of thirds works perfectly. This image of a singing male Prairie Warbler was made at Higbee's Beach WMA, Cape May, NJ.

Fuji Velvia pushed 1 stop, Canon FD 800mm f/5.6L lens & T-90 body, 50mm extension tube, center-weighted average metering at 0: 1/350 sec. at f/5.6.

Keep the Bird out of the Center of the Frame!

As you get closer and closer to your subject, the bird will take up a larger and larger portion of the frame; it becomes impossible to follow the rule of thirds. To achieve a pleasing composition, simply *keep the bird out of the center of the frame.* Leave more space in *front* of the bird (between the bill and the frame) than behind it (between the tail and the frame). By giving the bird room in the frame, your photograph will depict more of the bird's world as the bird sees it.

Head and Shoulders Portraits

Horizontal Format

When photographing large birds such as gulls, terns, or herons, you may get close enough to tame birds to take head and shoulders portraits. Such photographs present difficult problems in composition. Begin by centering the bird's eye and placing it at least halfway up in the frame, then—depending on the length of the bird's bill—adjust your composition until it looks pleasing to you.

The rules outlined above and all those that follow are not hard,

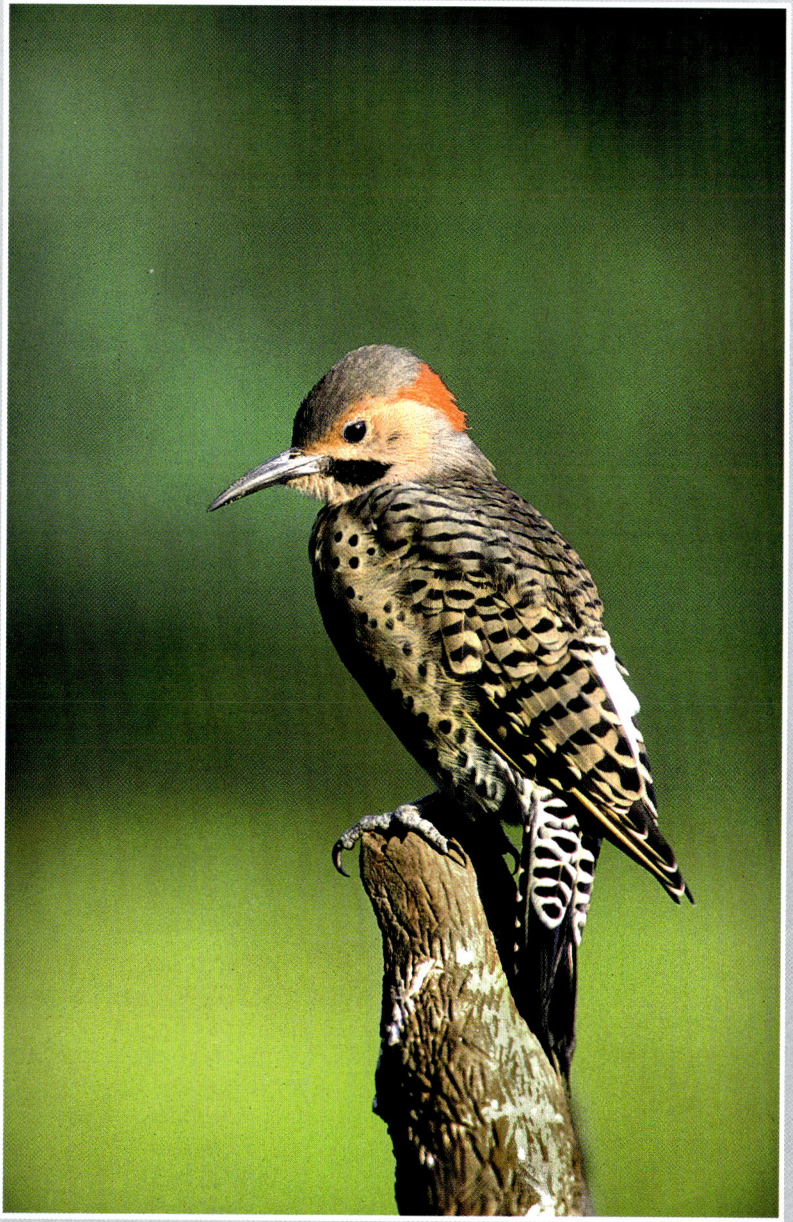

Working in vertical format, it is often best to center the subject from side to side and from top to bottom. At times it pays to leave a bit more space above the bird for the magazine title. This Northern Flicker was photographed at the Jamaica Bay Wildlife Refuge, Queens, NY.

Fuji Velvia, Canon FD 800mm f/5.6L lens & T-90 body, 50mm extension tube, center-weighted average metering at 0: 1/250 sec. at f/5.6.

fast rules, they are only guidelines. Once you have established your basic composition, move the bird slightly up or down in the frame, or shift it a bit to the left or right. You depress the shutter button. You are the artist.

Of course, there will be many times when you must compose, focus, and shoot in a matter of seconds. In these instances you must rely on both your experience and your artistic instincts to come up with a satisfactory composition.

Vertical Composition

Shooting verticals used to be very difficult, but many of today's camera bodies offer standard or optional vertical grips that make shooting verticals much easier. And using a double bubble level (see BIRDS AS ART under Suppliers) mounted in the camera's hot shoe (the slot that accepts the on-camera flash) will eliminate any alignment problems.

Several families of birds are best handled in vertical format. Cormorants, herons, egrets, bitterns, some long-legged shorebirds, most woodpeckers, and some perched raptors—all being tall, rather than long, fall into this category. Novice photographers, however, often try to stuff these tall birds into horizontal frames, rather than fitting them easily and pleasingly into vertical ones.

Rule of Thirds for Vertical Composition

When a bird—any bird, be it tall or long—is small in the frame, and you wish to use this composition, divide the frame in thirds from side to side, and in thirds from top to bottom. Place the subject at one of the four points of intersection. In more than a decade of photographing birds, I have taken less than a handful of images employing this composition; if a bird is small in the frame, I have found it easier to use a horizontal format (but may have passed up some good opportunities for making cover photographs).

Vertical Portraits

To achieve a pleasing vertical portrait, try this simple but oft-used composition: place the bird on the vertical centerline, equidistant from the top and bottom of the frame. You may wish to move the bird up or down a bit in the frame to include other compositional elements, or move it slightly closer to either vertical frame edge.

Head and Shoulders Portraits

Vertical Format

When shooting tight verticals of a bird's head, put the bird's eye or eyes on the vertical centerline about a third of the way down in the frame. Whether the bird is facing straight ahead or looking to the side, this will yield a good basic composition. You may—depending on the shape of the bird's neck and upper body and the length of its bill—wish to do some fine tuning.

Background Elements

If your subject is against an uncluttered background, or if there is a cluttered background many feet behind your subject, your telephoto lens, with its narrow angle of view and the shallow depth of field that comes with the use of wide apertures, will produce lovely, soft backgrounds. I'll take blue water—best on a still day, or well lit-green foliage every time.

When there are leaves and branches (or other background elements) on the same plane as your bird, these elements become integral background components. Depending on the configuration of these elements, and their positions relative to the subject, they may either ruin or enhance the image.

It is always best to avoid photographing birds against cluttered backgrounds. In many cases, you can eliminate distracting background elements by slowly changing *your* position by moving left or right, up or down. If a bright white seashell appears in your viewfinder just above a gull's back, you can hide the offending shell behind the bird by lowering your tripod a foot or two. When you are unable to clean up the background by changing your position, you'll need to wait for the gull to move—hopefully not to the next state.

Training yourself to actually *see* the background when you are focusing on an incredibly beautiful bird just yards away is a difficult task. By doing so, however, you will greatly improve the quality of your work.

Other Elements of Composition

The more you photograph birds, the more you will find yourself including various pebbles, rocks, boulders, blossoms, lily pads, leaves, logs, limbs, fences, fenceposts, pilings, and an assortment of other objects—both natural and man-made—in your work. By giving thought to the positioning of these objects in the frame and to the spatial relationship between these objects and your subjects, they can add to the compositional strength of your slides, rather than detract from it.

The spatial relationship between a bird and an object can change only if the bird shifts *its position.* You, however, can make the object appear to change *its position relative to the bird* by changing *your position* left or right, up or down. For example, if a distracting twig is located several inches behind the head of a perched landbird that is facing to your left, you can "move" the twig out from behind the bird by moving to *your* left.

• • •

Where *do* you put the bird? There are, of course, no right or wrong answers. Composition in bird photography is an art, not a science. But before you press the shutter button, keep the rules in mind and give this question some thought. The strength of your compositions, and the quality of your bird photographs, will increase dramatically.

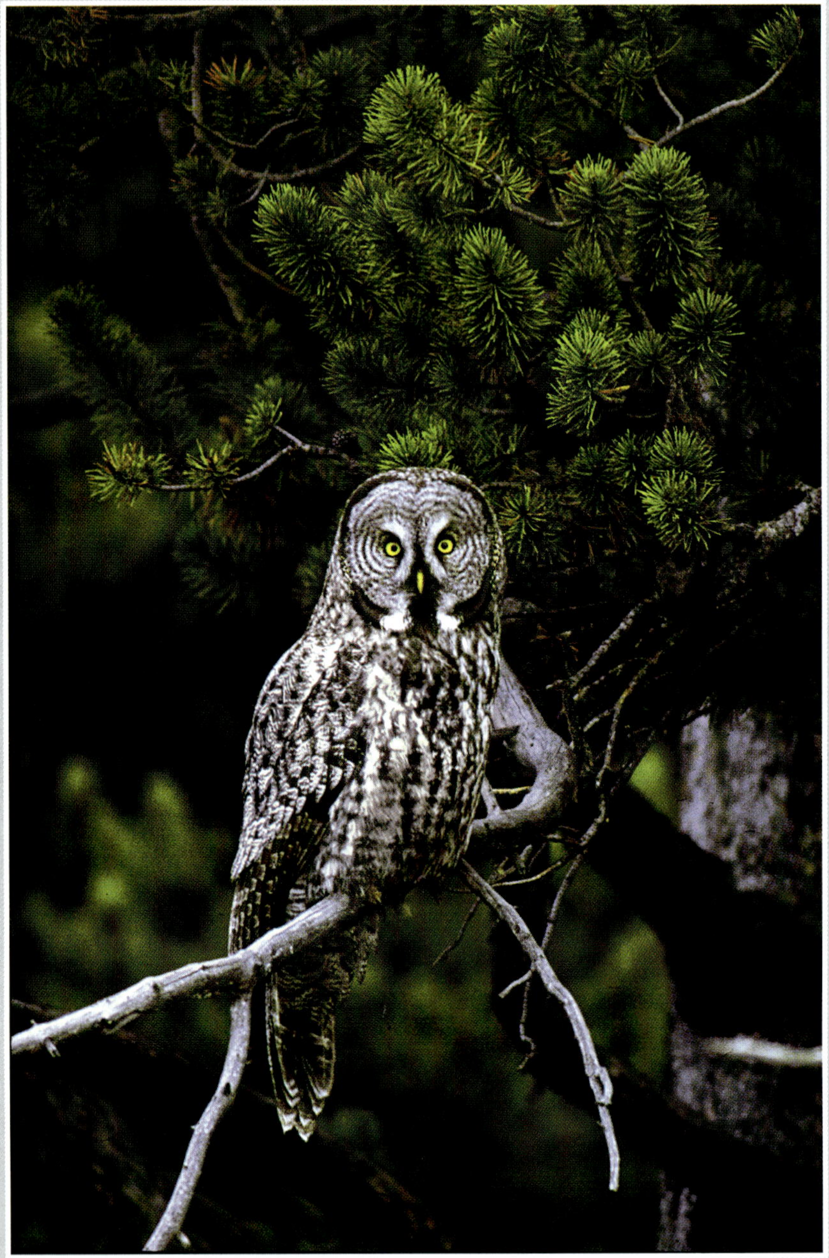

The evergreen background was perfect for this Great Gray Owl image made at Yellowstone National Park, WY. The gray trunk and branches helped frame the subject. Great grays are notoriously tame; I eventually got head shots of this beautiful owl.

Fuji Velvia pushed 1 stop, Canon FD 800mm lens & T-90 body, center-weighted average metering minus 1/3 stop: 1/45 sec. at f/5.6.

Chapter VIII

Getting Close

In 1983 I decided to become a bird photographer. I knew that spending hours, even days, in cramped blinds—the classic approach to bird photography—was not for me. I also knew that birds are wary, jittery, jumpy creatures, not easily approached. Undaunted, I set out. I knew nothing about photography, but with six years of intensive birding under my belt, I did know a lot about birds and bird behavior.

My initial attempts were pathetic at best; "Those dots on the slide, are they birds?" But I was determined to succeed. By spending lots of time in the field, observing, thinking, getting low, and moving slowly, I was soon able to get close to my subjects—without using a blind.

The Slow Approach

This sounds simple and it is. It works best with birds that are preoccupied: feeding, preening, bathing, even sleeping. After spotting a subject, take care when lifting your tripod-mounted telephoto rig off your shoulder prior to beginning your approach. Bend at the knees and ease the tripod onto the ground. (Slinging a tripod-mounted super-telephoto setup off your shoulder is *the* surest way that I know of to spook most birds.)

Now lift the entire rig, rest the camera back against your chest, and take a few steps. Pause, then take a few more. Slow down as you get closer. If the bird comes to alert posture, or sounds its alarm call, freeze. Continue to approach only when the bird becomes accustomed to your presence.

It is often best to take a few frames before reaching point-blank range. Photos taken at intermediate distances serve two purposes: they accustom the bird to the sound of the shutter and winder and they depict the bird's habitat far better than three-quarter frame shots. As you get closer, take only a step or two at a time, occasionally taking a few frames. Under the right conditions, the slow approach can result in head and shoulders portraits of your quarry. On bad days though, most birds will flush as you take your first step.

The Low Approach

The lower (and the slower), the better. With your tripod's legs suitably adjusted, carefully maneuver it in front of you while walking on your knees or waddling like a duck. On rocks and jetties, or when going down a slope, advance while seated. If you are on level ground, it may be best to crawl, marine-style, toward your subject.

With my manual focus 400mm lens, I mounted the rig in reverse on a Slik pan-tilt tripod head and shoved the locking handle into the mud for stability. With my two monster lenses, the 600 f/4 and the 800 f/5.6, I simply remove the lens from my tripod head, place the mounting foot of the lens (mounting plate and all) in the sand, dirt, or mud, and begin advancing.

Crawling can be wondrously effective on shorebirds, gulls, and terns, and can work well with other birds in flat, open areas. In most instances, the images attained while shooting at the bird's level are far more pleasing visually than those taken from above (or from below.)

Blinds

While I prefer to approach my subjects unconcealed and on foot, there are times when it is desirable, even necessary, to use a blind. It is often impossible to approach and photograph notoriously shy and skittish birds like ibises, grouse, larks, and longspurs without being hidden in a blind. Using a blind can reduce stress on nesting birds.

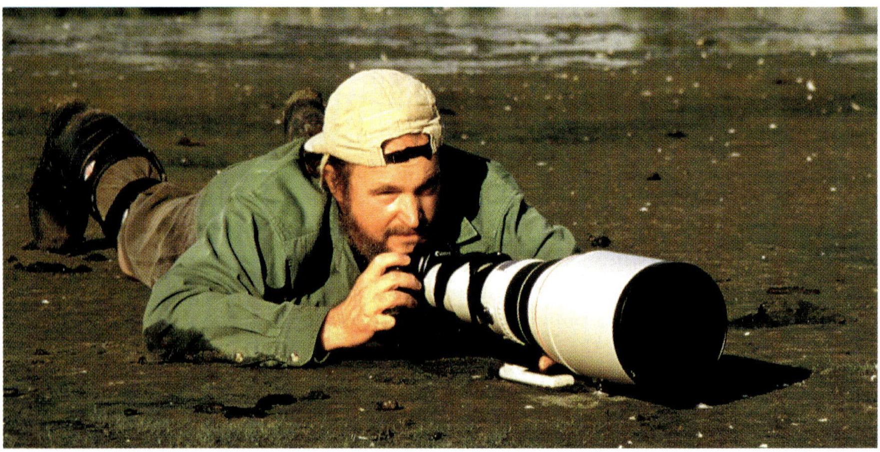

The author, with his Canon EF 600mm f/4 lens, in pursuit of his beloved shorebirds at Jamaica Bay, Queens, NY. Photo courtesy of Milton Heiberg.

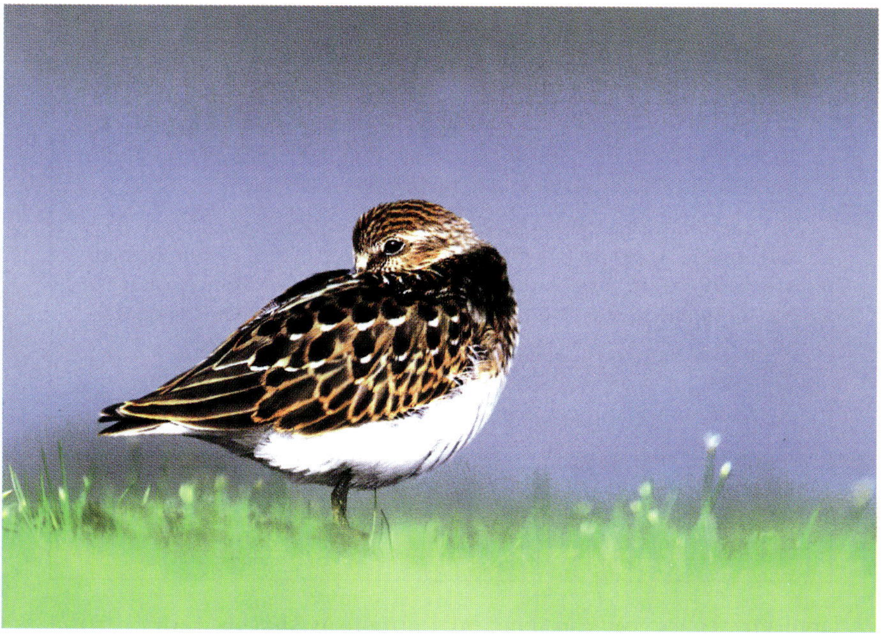

Getting down and dirty can yield almost surrealistic images. This juvenile Least Sandpiper slept peacefully at the Jamaica Bay Wildlife Refuge, Queens, NY.

Fuji Velvia pushed 1 stop, EF Canon 600mm f/4.0L lens & EOS 1N body, 1.4X tele-extender, Evaluative metering plus 1/3 stop: 1/640 sec. at f/5.6.

Permanent blinds, usually fixed wooden structures, are often built adjacent to ponds or feeding stations, or at strategic locations in seabird colonies. In many cases, they offer consistently good, if not consistently spectacular photographic opportunities.

Portable blinds made from tear-proof fabric on foldable frames are available from several suppliers. They can be easily carried into the field and set up quickly in desirable locations. They usually require the use of a small stool or folding chair and are almost always quite cramped.

Bag blinds, which are large cloth covers with eyeholes and lens cutouts or sleeves, can be quite effective. You can sew one yourself from several square yards of camouflage cloth, or purchase one; Rod Planck and DB Design (see Suppliers) both offer excellent models.

When you find a spot where roosting birds flush upon your approach and return quickly when you back off, you will want to use your bag blind. Drape the blind over yourself and your outfit and slowly maneuver into position. Even if the birds flush, it is likely that they will return quickly.

Makeshift blinds can, in a pinch, be jury-rigged from a great variety of materials, including large

Ethical Considerations and Field Behavior

Bird photographers need be aware that their actions can have adverse effects on both the birds that they are attempting to photograph and the environment that their subjects inhabit.

Study your subjects well. Learn their body language. Learn their tolerances. Approach a bird once, twice, three times. If your attempts are unsuccessful, find another subject. And take extreme care when photographing birds at the nest or birds that are resting or sleeping.

In parks and refuges know and follow the rules. Stay on the path if indicated. Be careful when traversing fragile habitat. And respect the rights of other photographers and birders.

Initiate discussions of field ethics at camera clubs, photographic associations, natural history societies, and with photographer friends. In the field, think before you act: "How will my actions effect the birds, the environment, and others?"

appliance boxes (you can stand in a refrigerator carton), canvases, drop cloths, tents and tent poles, ladders, broom handles, steel rods, broken branches and dead vegetation, and rope, gaffer's tape, or wire (to hold everything together).

Using your car as a blind can be a great way to get close to birds and other wildlife. This technique is especially productive when visiting refuges that have auto tour routes where the birds are accustomed to vehicles. You can set up your tripod in the car, or simply support your outfit on a pillow or beanbag resting on a partially lowered window.

Best, though, is the Groofwin (ground/roof/window) Pod, a strong, stable, window mount (see Leonard Lee Rue Enterprises in Suppliers). When used in conjunction with a quality ball-head, consistently sharp images result. And fatigue is sharply reduced; the mount, not *you*, supports the lens during long shooting sessions.

With your lens suitably supported, drive slowly up to your subject and turn off the engine to eliminate vibration. Then frame, focus, and fire away.

The Thinking Photographer

With careful observation, imaginative thinking, patience, and determination, you can take advantage of countless photographic opportunities that others overlook. Birds flushed inadvertently, or while being approached, will at times quickly and repeatedly return to preferred perches, roosting sites, favored feeding areas, rainwater pools, abandoned prey, or partially scavenged carcasses.

Do not lament when a bird shows you its tail feathers. Get as low as possible. Position your tripod. Remain motionless. In a matter of minutes you may be rewarded with a once-in-a-lifetime photographic opportunity.

There are hundreds of situations that are tailor-made for the bird photographer. Here are just a few: Flocks of shorebirds roosting in the lee of a dune, or crouching in fear of falcons overhead, may refuse to fly. Boats returning to fishing stations and commercial fish docks can attract hundreds of gulls and terns in late afternoon as the day's catch is being cleaned or processed. Drakes of various wild species often mingle with eager Mallards at duck-feeding ponds in winter.

Gulls, terns, shorebirds, and cormorants become acclimated to the human presence after hundreds of dog walkers, surfers, tidepooling tourists, sunbathers, shell collectors, and fishermen walk by them each day without causing undue havoc. And small landbirds singing from exposed perches will defend their territories even against 500mm lenses. Look. See. Think. Shoot.

Little Do They Know

At times, a particular bird may allow a particular photographer great freedom, as if the bird were a model being paid by the hour. Onlookers, and often the photographers

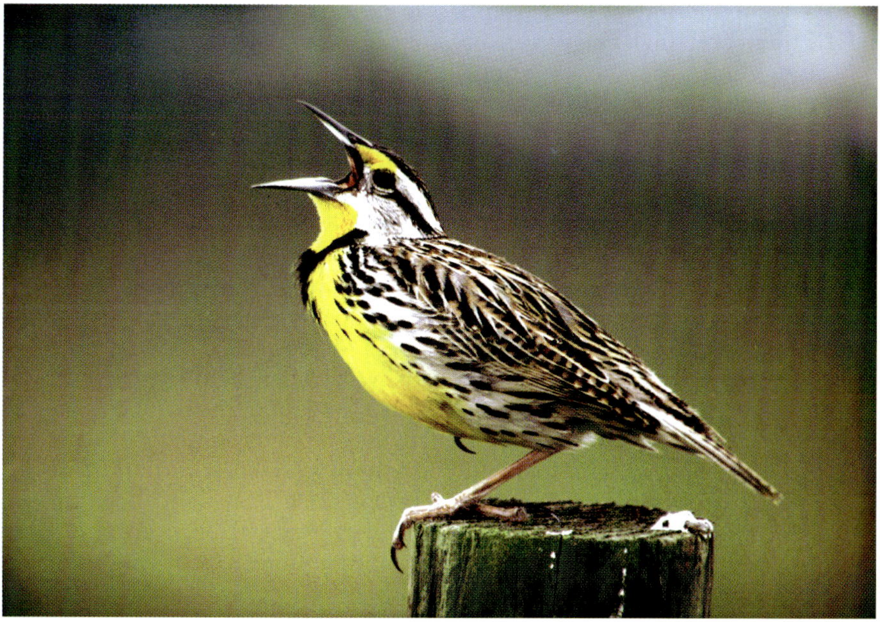

A pillow resting on a lowered car window provided support for the 800mm lens used to make this image of a singing Eastern Meadowlark at Old Venus, FL.

Kodachrome 64, Canon FD 800mm lens, 50mm extension tube, & T-90 body, center-weighted average metering at zero: 1/60 sec. at f/5.6.

themselves, are amazed. The possible explanations for such cooperative behavior are many; understanding them can improve your chances immeasurably.

Most juvenile birds make good subjects—some are astoundingly tame. (Young birds of many species are easily distinguished by their evenly patterned upperparts, each feather distinctively fringed buff or white.) Newly arrived migrants from arctic regions may never have seen humans before, so they, too, often make wonderful subjects.

Weary, hungry migrants—their occurrences often storm related—are often so intent on resting, or on feeding ravenously, that they are oblivious to all else. Birds summering far to the south of their breeding ranges can be sitting ducks, or loons, or grebes, or scoters. Though sick or injured birds are often easily approached, the resulting photos are usually, but not always, disappointing.

In Your Backyard

If you are clever, photographing birds in your backyard allows you far more control over subject position, lighting angle, foreground and background elements, and even the bird's choice of perch than you could ever hope for in the wild. If your backyard is not blessed with bountiful berry-bearing bushes, thick tangles, and a small, noisy stream, you can easily introduce food, shelter, and water into the open spaces around your home. There is a profusion of excellent books on attracting birds to your backyard.

Bird photographers, however, should use the suggestions in these books as starting points, and then adapt them to meet their photographic needs. Even those blessed with mini-wildlife refuges as backyards may wish to do some replanting and a bit of trimming to custom-tailor their property for bird photography. In setting up your backyard for bird photography, planning is the key. I have seen countless feeders rife with birds that were practically useless for photography. Deep shade is usually the chief culprit. Feeders (or bird baths or water drips) should be placed so that they are lit by morning or afternoon sunlight.

In some situations, it is possible to position a single feeder or water feature so that it is lit by both morning and afternoon light. In most cases, though, two positions are necessary. Hanging feeders or water drips can simply be moved from one spot to another. Platform feeders or bird baths that get only morning light can be covered around noon, at which time afternoon feeders and baths are uncovered. Making these changes on a daily basis will help the birds to quickly adapt to the pattern.

Before determining the exact location of a feeder, it is important to consider where and how the *photographer* will be positioned. Many questions must be answered: How long a lens will you be using? What is its minimum focusing distance—with and without extension tubes? Will you be standing, seated, or prone? Will you be shooting from an open house window, or concealed in a blind? (There's a lot to be said for just remaining still in plain sight, as most feeder birds quickly become accustomed to the human presence.)

If the birds ignore the perfect perch that you have erected, and persist, instead, in landing on an obstructed natural perch at the edge of your yard (most birds have a favorite), clip a few branches here and there. In a National Wildlife Refuge this is a federal offense, but in your own backyard, it is called "pruning."

There is no doubt about it, specifically tailoring *your* backyard to fit *your* photographic needs will present you with a great many opportunities to produce quality images.

Some Dos and Don'ts

- *Do* wear a cap on windy days; at close range blowing hair can scare birds.
- *Don't* feel that it's necessary to wear camouflage clothing.
- *Do* wear your scroungiest attire. After you've been crawling in black muck, *don't* forget to hose yourself off *before* going into the house.
- *Do* remove the camera strap to prevent camera strap-flap.
- *Don't* begin your approach without putting several rolls of extra film in your pockets.
- *Never* lift your tripod-mounted long lens quickly off your shoulder when you are close to a bird or birds; for some reason, this is as threatening to most birds as if your were raising a shotgun. *Always* take your tripod-mounted telephoto lens off your shoulder well before you get into range and lift it in front of you as you advance.
- *Do*, if possible, keep trees, bushes, utility poles, and even buildings, between yourself and the bird while approaching. (When you pass such objects, keep them directly *behind* you to help "kill" your silhouette.)
- *Don't* leave home without extension tubes—you'll soon be getting so close to the birds that you'll need them to reduce your lens's minimum focusing distance. *Never* make rapid movements. *Always* be prepared; you never can tell when a photogenic bird will decide to land right in front of you for no reason at all!

The Easy Way Out

Fly to Florida. Rent a car. Traverse the wildlife drive at Ding Darling National Wildlife Refuge on Sanibel Island or visit the Anhinga Trail in Everglades National Park. And bring lots of film.

Getting close to wild birds with a camera and a long lens can be difficult. It can be frustrating. It can be deeply disappointing. But the rewards are sweet. Natural moments from the lives of wild creatures are preserved on film, to be enjoyed in solitude or shared with others. Photographers share not only these frozen moments in time, but also—in a personal way—the very lives of the birds they photograph, their environment, and their beauty.

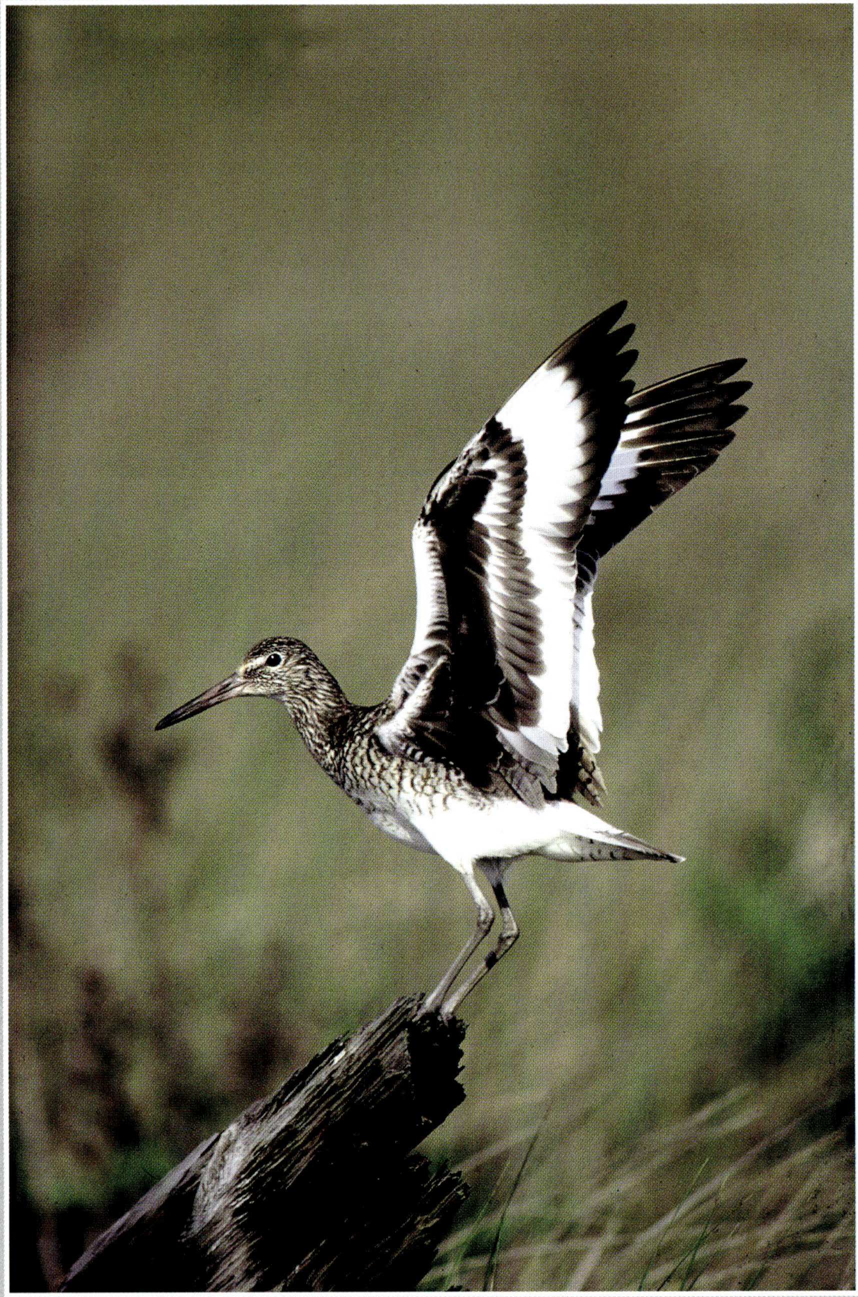

Do not attempt to conserve film when shooting action and behavior. This Willet image, taken on Long Island, New York, was clearly the best in a series of more than 20 exposures.

Fuji Velvia, Canon FD 800mm f/5.6L lens & T-90 body. Sunny 16 minus 1/2 stop: 1/500 at f/5.6.

Chapter IX

Photographing Action and Behavior

Though a well-composed, technically perfect portrait of a perched bird doing absolutely nothing at all may make a fine image, a photo of the same bird calling, yawning, tipping, crouching in fear, stretching, ruffling its feathers, eating, taking flight, flapping, soaring, or even just sleeping will almost always be more interesting.

There are countless instances when your knowledge of bird behavior can help you anticipate what will happen next. Sleeping birds often yawn upon awakening; after ruffling their feathers, they will often stretch a wing to the side. A bird that has stretched one wing will almost always stretch the other wing next, and one that tips forward will usually stretch both wings elegantly overhead and then take flight. Shorebirds often glance skyward to check for predators. After photographing this behavior, look up; you might get a flight shot of a falcon. Dive-bombing crows can lead you to raptors as well. Be ready to shoot on cue.

When Unexpected Action Occurs, Shoot!

If you are zeroed in on a bird and it does something unexpected, fire the shutter immediately. Do not attempt to change the aperture or shutter speed; the action will be over before you finish making your adjustments—it may be over *before* you begin. By shooting *when* the action occurs, you give yourself a chance to capture it on film.

Dinner Time

When photographing feeding birds, try to capture as many steps in the process as possible. Forag-

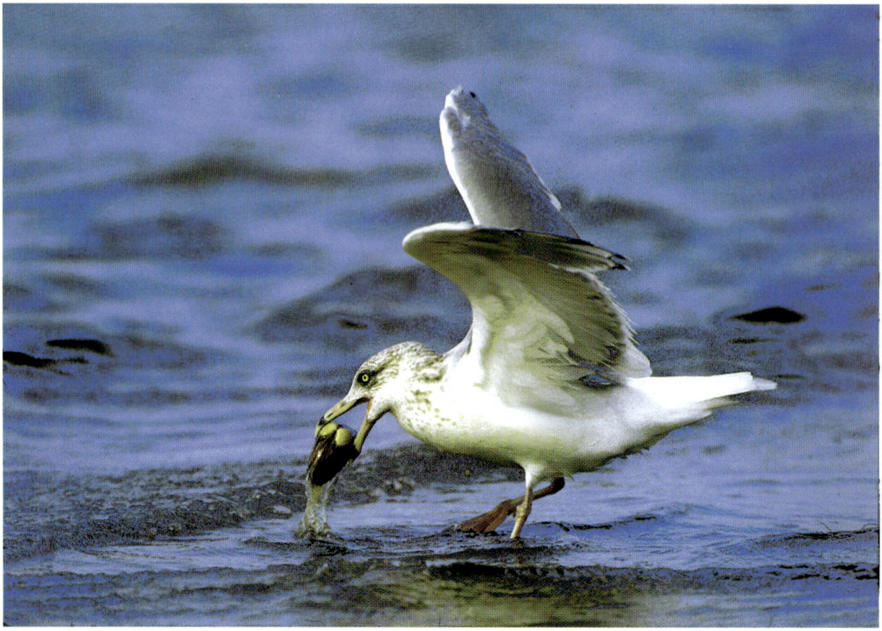

The more time that you spend observing birds, the greater your chance of figuring out what they will do next. This Herring Gull extracted its lunch, a surf clam, at Stone Harbor Point, NJ.

Fuji Velvia pushed 1 stop, Canon EF 600mm f/4.0L lens & EOS 1N body, 1.4X tele-extender, Evaluative metering at 0: 1/750 sec. at f/5.6.

ing, grazing, picking, probing, plucking, dabbling, diving, and stalking, attacking, capturing, holding, subduing, and swallowing prey are among the possibilities. Additionally, most large herons and egrets take a drink immediately after downing a large meal.

Too Close

When attempting to photograph bird behavior, or a bird in action, it is very important not to get *too* close to your subject. If you do, and the bird moves or stretches, some part of the bird may be cut off by the edge of the frame.

When photographing birds involved in territorial disputes, it is especially important to give yourself enough working room; their movements are often rapid and violent. Breeding gulls, for example, are busy defending their territories from late winter through spring and often engage in fierce battles.

By resisting the urge to get closer while photographing aggressive behaviors, you will find it easier to follow the action, to keep the birds in the frame, and to focus. Select one of the combatants and focus on its eye. If you are using autofocus, it is best (if possible) to choose an outside sensor and attempt to maintain focus on *one* of the subjects.

If you are working on a tripod, loosen all tripod head controls so that you can follow the action easily; the tripod will give you the vertical support that you need. With short or intermediate telephotos, however, it is far easier to follow birds in flight and in action when hand-holding your outfit than when working on a tripod.

Be Patient; Take Advantage of Your Good Chances

When you get close to a wild bird without disturbing it, you will often be able to photograph it for an extended period of time. Remain still and keep your eye glued to the viewfinder; be assured that the instant you take your eye away from the viewfinder, the bird *will* do something spectacular. By being patient, you can capture an interesting series of photographs of the same bird exhibiting a variety of behaviors.

In Closing

Taking good photographs that depict bird behavior, birds in flight, and birds in action is difficult. It requires persistence, patience, and a working knowledge of both photography and bird behavior.

Many, if not most or all of your slides may wind up in the trash can. Yet, aside from the occasional astonishing image, there are many other rewards. Moments spent with a preening peep or with a heron struggling to swallow a huge fish are not soon forgotten. You will witness some behaviors that many ornithologists would have trouble explaining, and others that may never have been seen before—by anyone. If you're lucky—and determined—you *will* get your pictures.

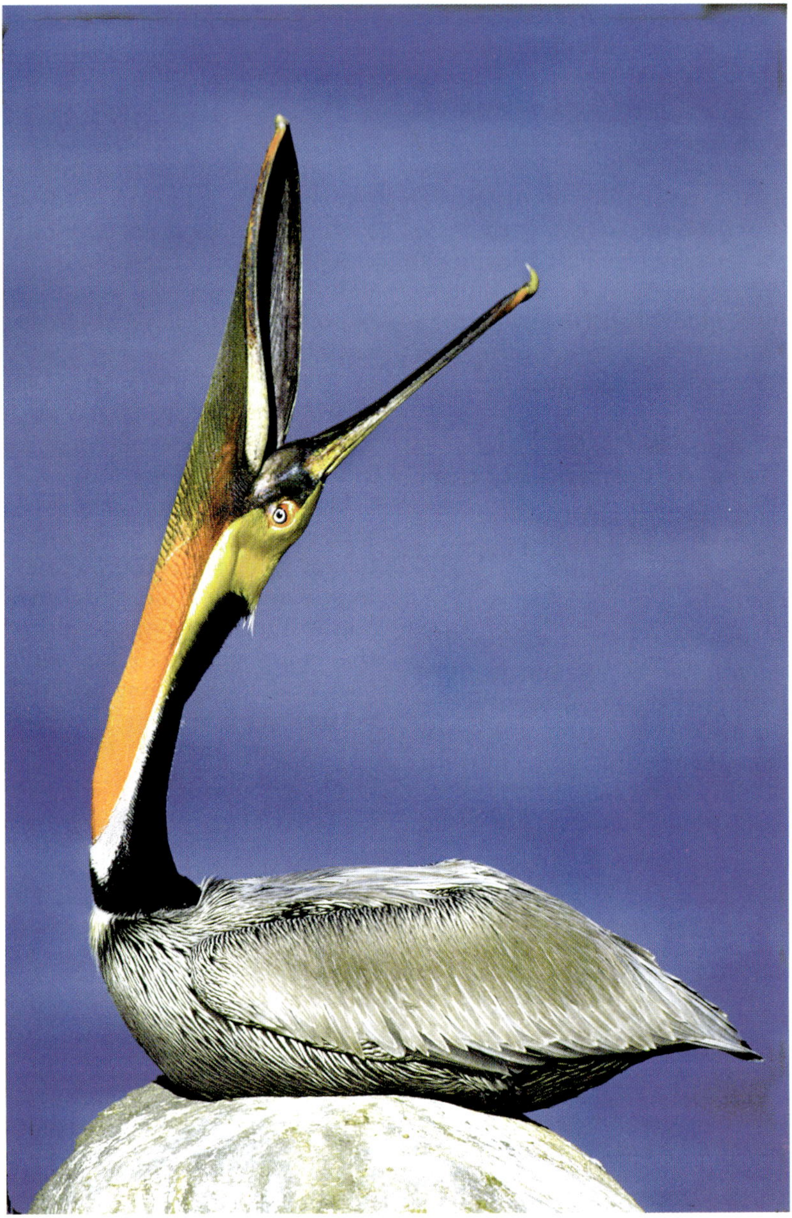

A Brown Pelican's head-throw is thought to be a form of intra-flock communication. I framed this shot, made at La Jolla, California, so that the bird's head and bill were nearly out of the lower left corner of the frame and waited for the bird to do its thing.

Fuji Velvia pushed 1 stop, Canon EF 600mm f/4.0L lens & EOS 1N body, Evaluative metering at 0: 1/2000 sec. at f/4.

Selected Suppliers

Arthur Morris/BIRDS AS ART
1455 Whitewood Drive
Deltona, FL 32725
(407) 860-2013

Instructional Photo-Tours
Better Beamer Flash Extenders
Double Bubble Levels

Chelsea Professional Color Lab
Att: Sheetal Kumar, Mgr.
159 West 27th Street
New York, NY 10001
(212) 229-2929

E-6 Processing, 35mm and 70mm
Reproduction Quality Duplicates

DB Design
P.O. Box 1571
Forestville, CA 95436

Portable Blinds
Progrips for Nikon
8008 and 8008s

Erie Color Slide Club
P.O. Box 672
Erie, PA 16512-0672
(814) 456-7578

Cardboard crop mounts

Franklin Distributors Corp
P.O. Box 320
Denville, NJ 07834
(201) 267-2710

Archival Storage Materials

Leonard Lee Rue Enterprises
136 Millbrook Road
Blairstown, NJ 07825
(908) 362-6616

Photographic Accessories
Groofwin Pods, Vests
Nature and Photo Books

M & M Photo Source, Ltd.
1135 37th Street
Brooklyn, NY 11218
(800) 606-6746

Cameras, Lenses, Tripods
Ball-heads, Film

B. Moose Peterson
P.O. Box 3628
Mammoth Lakes, CA 93546-3628

Lowepro Pro Trekker AW:
All-Weather Super-Telephoto
Backpack (Airline Friendly)

Rod Planck Photography
P.O. Box 169
Paradise, MI 49768
(906) 492-3444

Bag Blinds, Reflectors
Diffusers, Workshops
Nature and Photo Books

Really Right Stuff
Att: Bryan Geyer
P.O. Box 6531
Los Osos, CA 93412
(805) 528-6321

Photographic Accessories:
Quick Release Plates
Flash Brackets

Sun Precautions, Inc.
2815 Wetmore Avenue
Everett, WA 98201
(800) 882-7860

Sun Protective Clothing

The Slideprinter
P.O.Box 9506
Denver, CO 80209-9969
(303) 698-2962

Prints From Slides

The Stock Solution
Salt Lake City, UT 84101
(800) 777-2076, Ext. 5

Fold Mats for 70mm Dupes
Self-Sealing 35mm Mounts

Wimberley Design
133 Bryarly Road
Winchester, VA 22603
(703) 665-2744

Wimberley Tripod Head
for Super-telephoto Lenses